Prepper's Guide to End Times

Surviving the Unthinkable

David Dean

Prepper's Guide to End Times

1.
2.
3.
4.
5.
6.
7.
8.
9.
10.
11.
12.
13.

Chapter One

Introduction

In an age where our lives are cushioned by technological advancements and modern conveniences, it is easy to forget that the world is inherently unpredictable. Natural disasters strike without warning, economies crumble under unforeseen pressures, and societal structures can unravel in mere moments. The facade of stability we rely on is fragile, and beneath it lies a reality that requires us to be vigilant and prepared. For those who seek to fortify themselves against these uncertainties, this book stands as a beacon of knowledge and resilience.

Imagine waking up one day to find the world you know has been turned upside down. Perhaps it's a devastating earthquake that has reduced your city to rubble, or maybe it's an economic collapse that has left banks empty and store shelves barren. In such scenarios, the familiar comforts of everyday life vanish, replaced by a stark struggle for survival. It is in these moments that preparedness becomes not just a choice, but a necessity. This book aims to guide you through this essential journey, equipping you with the skills and strategies needed to navigate extreme situations.

The concept of prepping is often misunderstood, dismissed by some as unnecessary paranoia. However, true preparedness goes beyond stockpiling food and supplies; it encompasses a mindset of adaptability and self-reliance. This mindset transforms daunting challenges into manageable tasks, allowing you to face uncertainty with confidence and clarity. As you turn these pages, you will discover that prepping is not about fear—it's about empowerment. It's about taking control of your destiny in a world that can change in an instant.

From the deserts stripped bare by droughts to the coastal areas battered by hurricanes, history shows us countless examples of environments that have tested human resilience. These events serve as reminders of our vulnerability and the importance of readiness. Yet, prepping isn't solely about surviving immediate threats; it's about fostering long-term resilience. Our journey together will explore the multifaceted nature of preparedness, weaving through practical advice, proven techniques, and tales of those who have faced adversity head-on.

Consider this book as your roadmap through the unpredictable landscape of potential crises. Just as a seasoned traveler packs essentials for the journey ahead, you too will learn to prepare for the unknown. We'll start with the basics—understanding the types of emergencies you might face and identifying the initial steps to take. Gradually, we'll delve deeper into more nuanced strategies, from creating emergency plans tailored to your unique circumstances to honing skills that will serve you in any situation.

Prepping involves more than just physical preparation. Your mental fortitude will play an equally critical role in ensuring your survival and well-being. You'll learn how to cultivate a resilient mindset, capable of weathering the psychological toll of prolonged crises. Whether you're dealing with panic-induced chaos in the wake of a disaster or maintaining morale during extended periods of instability, mental strength will be your greatest ally.

A key aspect of successful prepping is community. No man is an island, and in times of crisis, the support of others can make all the difference. You will be guided on how to build and maintain networks of like-minded individuals, fostering a sense of solidarity that amplifies your collective strength. From sharing resources to coordinating efforts, the bonds you form can enhance your chances of thriving rather than merely surviving.

Throughout this book, you will also encounter discussions on cutting-edge tools and technologies that can aid in your quest for preparedness. While traditional methods hold timeless value, modern innovations offer new dimensions of efficiency and effectiveness. Balancing time-tested wisdom with contemporary advancements will give you a well-rounded approach to preparing for any eventuality.

As we venture further, you'll find specialized chapters dedicated to different aspects of prepping, each designed to expand your skill set and deepen your understanding. Learn how to secure your home against various threats, master the art of first aid, and develop sustainable food sources. Each topic is meticulously crafted to provide you with actionable insights, transforming theoretical knowledge into practical application.

Remember, the purpose of this book is not to instill fear but to inspire action. We live in a world where planning for potential adversities is a mark of prudence, not pessimism. By the end of this journey, you will emerge not just as a survivor, but as someone equipped to thrive, no matter what fate may throw your way. The skills you gain here will be versatile, adaptable, and applicable to a wide range of scenarios, empowering you to face the future with a calm and prepared mind.

So, whether you're a seasoned prepper looking to refine your strategies or a newcomer seeking a comprehensive introduction to the art of preparedness, this book is your guide. Embrace the journey of becoming more self-reliant and resilient. Equip yourself with the knowledge that has the power to transform fear into confidence, chaos into order, and uncertainty into opportunity. Together, let's embark on this path towards preparedness, arming ourselves with the wisdom and tools necessary to navigate and endure whatever challenges lie ahead.

Chapter Two

Understanding the End Times

Understanding the end times is a complex journey through various catastrophic events, historical collapses, and their psychological impacts. This chapter delves into the profound ways in which natural disasters, man-made catastrophes, pandemics, and geopolitical turmoil have shaped societies throughout history. By examining these phenomena, we aim to uncover patterns and lessons that can guide our preparations for future disruptions.

The chapter unfolds with an exploration of different types of catastrophic events that have disrupted society at its core. It highlights how natural disasters, like earthquakes and hurricanes, cause immediate societal breakdowns, while man-made catastrophes, such as nuclear accidents and terrorist attacks, have long-lasting impacts on social structures. Subsequently, the focus shifts to historical examples of societal collapse, drawing parallels between past civilizations and modern-day challenges. The discussion extends to the psychological impacts of disasters, analyzing trauma responses and the importance of community resilience. Through this examination, readers will gain insights into the interconnected nature of these elements and learn strategies to mitigate risks and enhance resilience, ultimately preparing for potential future crises.

Types of Catastrophic Events

Catastrophic events have the potential to disrupt society at its core, leading to immediate and long-term consequences. Understanding these events can help us prepare for future disruptions and mitigate their impacts.

Natural Disasters

Natural disasters such as earthquakes, hurricanes, and wildfires can lead to immediate societal breakdown. Earthquakes, for example, can devastate infrastructure within minutes, leaving people without homes, utilities, or medical care. The 2010 earthquake in Haiti is a stark reminder of how quickly a country's social fabric can unravel. With over 200,000 lives lost and millions made homeless, the aftermath saw chaos and a breakdown in law and order. Hurricanes, like Hurricane Katrina in 2005, demonstrate similar destructive power. Katrina overwhelmed emergency services, led to massive displacement, and left lasting scars on New Orleans' economy and community. Wildfires, becoming increasingly common due to climate change, also exemplify this impact. The 2019-2020

Australian wildfires destroyed thousands of homes and strained community resources.

Man-made Catastrophes

Man-made catastrophes include nuclear accidents and terrorist attacks, which can severely impact social structures. The Chernobyl disaster in 1986 resulted not only in immediate deaths and health issues but also in long-term environmental and social consequences. The exclusion zone around Chernobyl remains uninhabitable, disrupting local communities. Similarly, the Fukushima nuclear disaster in Japan in 2011 displaced over 150,000 people and had lasting impacts on public trust in government and technology. Terrorist attacks, such as those on September 11, 2001, in the United States, show how a single event can alter national policies, economic stability, and social cohesion. Post-9/11, there was an increase in security measures, changes in foreign policy, and a rise in societal fear and division. These examples illustrate that man-made catastrophes can reshape societies in profound ways.

Pandemics

Pandemics, such as COVID-19, have far-reaching implications for societal stability. The rapid spread of the virus caused global health crises, overwhelming healthcare systems, and leading to unprecedented lockdowns. Economically, businesses shuttered, unemployment soared, and governments had to roll out massive relief packages. Socially, the pandemic exposed and exacerbated existing inequalities, from access to healthcare to job security. Historically, the Spanish Flu of 1918 offers another perspective, killing millions globally and leading to similar disruptions. Pandemics strain not just healthcare but also mental health, with increased rates of anxiety, depression, and other conditions. Through such experiences, we see how pandemics can fundamentally challenge societal norms and operations.

Geopolitical Turmoil

Geopolitical turmoil, including conflicts, wars, and political upheavals, can plunge societies into disarray. Wars often displace populations, destroy infrastructure, and create refugee crises. For instance, the Syrian Civil War, ongoing since 2011, has led to widespread destruction, with millions fleeing the country and many more internally displaced. This conflict has strained neighboring countries and created complex international political challenges. Political upheavals can be equally destabilizing. The Arab Spring, a series of anti-government protests across the Arab world starting in 2010, demonstrates how quickly political instability can arise and result in power vacuums, civil unrest, and economic collapse. Countries like Egypt and Libya faced tumultuous transitions that disrupted everyday life and governance. Geopolitical conflicts like these show that political instability can be as disruptive as natural disasters or pandemics.

Historical Examples of Societal Collapse

Learning from past instances of societal collapse to understand potential future scenarios is crucial for both preparedness and mitigation. By examining the factors that led to the fall of historical civilizations, we can draw valuable lessons applicable to our contemporary world.

The collapse of civilizations such as the Roman Empire and the Mayan culture offers a wealth of knowledge about the delicate balance required to maintain a thriving society. The Roman Empire, for instance, encountered several challenges that led to its downfall. Among these were political instability, economic troubles, and military defeats. The once sprawling empire, covering millions of square kilometers, experienced a significant reduction in size and influence over a short period (Kemp, 2019). The Mayan civilization, known for its advanced architectural achievements and complex writing system, similarly found itself unable to sustain its societal model amid environmental pressures and internal conflict.

Understanding the specific role of environmental, social, and political factors in societal collapses provides insight into the interconnected nature of these elements. Environmental changes, such as prolonged droughts, have often precipitated societal collapse by undermining agricultural productivity and leading to food shortages. The Anasazi people are a prime example of this phenomenon; their society disintegrated under the strain of environmental stresses, leading to widespread abandonment of settlements.

Social inequality and political corruption have also played pivotal roles in the downfall of societies. As wealth and power become concentrated among a small elite, social cohesion diminishes. This can lead to civil unrest and weaken a society's ability to respond to crises. Historical evidence suggests that excessive inequality contributed to the collapse of the Western Roman Empire, where the disparity between the wealthy elite and the impoverished masses grew unsustainable.

Drawing parallels between historical events and contemporary challenges allows us to recognize patterns and take preemptive action. Current global issues, such as climate change, resource depletion, and political fragmentation, mirror many of the conditions that led to past collapses. For example, modern societies face the threat of climate-induced disasters, similar to those that affected ancient civilizations. Rising sea levels, frequent hurricanes, and extended droughts can erode infrastructure, reduce agricultural output, and displace populations, creating a cascade of problems that challenge social stability.

Moreover, the theory of "normal accidents" posits that complex technological systems are inherently susceptible to failure (Kemp, 2019). This insight underscores the vulnerability of our highly interconnected and technologically dependent societies. While technological advancements offer numerous benefits, they also introduce new risks and points of failure. The global financial crisis of 2008 serves as a contemporary example of how systemic weaknesses can lead to widespread disruption.

Modern crises provide further context for understanding societal breakdowns. Economic collapses, for instance, highlight the fragility of financial systems and their critical role in maintaining societal stability. The 2001 collapse of Argentina's economy resulted in widespread unemployment, poverty, and social unrest. The subsequent erosion of public trust in government institutions exacerbated the country's difficulties, illustrating how economic decline can trigger a broader societal crisis.

Failed states offer another lens through which to examine modern societal collapses. Countries like Somalia and Venezuela have experienced profound breakdowns in governance, leading to lawlessness, economic hardship, and mass displacement. These cases demonstrate the consequences of weakened state structures and emphasize the importance of effective governance in preventing societal collapse.

By studying these historical and modern examples, we can identify key indicators of impending societal distress. Monitoring factors such as environmental degradation, economic inequality, and political instability allows us to develop strategies to mitigate risks and enhance resilience. Proactive measures, including sustainable resource management, equitable economic policies, and transparent governance, are essential to avert potential collapses.

Psychological Impact of Disasters

In times of catastrophic events, the emotional and psychological toll on individuals and communities can be profound. Understanding these impacts is crucial for preparing and implementing effective responses to future crises. By delving into the nature of trauma response, analyzing the long-term effects of trauma, examining community resilience, and discussing strategies for building psychological strength, we can better comprehend the mental health challenges posed by disasters and how to address them.

Traumatic events such as natural disasters, pandemics, or large-scale accidents often trigger a range of psychological responses. Anxiety, fear, and post-traumatic stress disorder (PTSD) are common reactions among those affected. Individuals may experience overwhelming feelings of hopelessness, helplessness, and extreme fear. The sudden and unexpected nature of disasters disrupts the sense of safety and stability, leading to acute stress responses. These symptoms can manifest immediately following the event or emerge weeks to months later, impacting daily functioning and overall well-being.

The impact of trauma extends beyond the immediate aftermath. Long-term effects on mental health can persist for years, influencing various aspects of an individual's life. Chronic anxiety, depression, and PTSD are frequent outcomes that can significantly hinder one's ability to lead a normal life. Persistent sleep disturbances, flashbacks, and intrusive thoughts are symptoms that survivors may endure. Studies show that the intensity and duration of these symptoms can vary widely among individuals, depending on factors such as the severity of the event, personal resilience, and the level of available social support (Makwana, 2019).

Community resilience plays a pivotal role in mitigating the adverse effects of disasters. Following a catastrophic event, communities often come together to provide mutual support and aid. This collective effort fosters a sense of solidarity and shared purpose, which can be a powerful antidote to the isolation and despair felt by individuals. Initiatives such as community rebuilding projects, support groups, and local resource networks are vital components of this resilience. They not only offer practical assistance but also reinforce social bonds, creating an environment where individuals feel supported and understood.

Building resilience and psychological strength is essential for preparing individuals and communities for future disasters. Mental health education and awareness programs can equip people with the tools to recognize and manage stressors effectively. Training in psychological first aid, for instance, empowers community members to offer initial support to those affected by trauma. Additionally, fostering a culture that prioritizes mental health can reduce stigma and encourage individuals to seek help when needed.

One effective approach to bolstering resilience is through mindfulness and stress-reduction techniques. Practices such as meditation, deep-breathing exercises, and yoga can help individuals regulate their emotions and reduce anxiety levels. These practices promote self-awareness and emotional regulation, enabling people to better cope with stress and adversity. Incorporating these techniques into daily routines can build mental resilience over time.

Another critical aspect of resilience-building involves strengthening social connections. Strong relationships with family, friends, and community members provide a vital support network during times of crisis. Initiatives that promote social cohesion, such as community gatherings, volunteer opportunities, and peer support groups, can enhance these connections. By nurturing these relationships, individuals have a reliable source of emotional and practical support to draw upon during emergencies.

Preparedness training is also a crucial element of resilience. Educating individuals about potential disaster scenarios and providing clear action plans can reduce panic and confusion during actual events. Practical skills such as first aid, emergency communication, and evacuation procedures can empower individuals to act decisively and confidently in the face of danger. Simulation exercises and drills can further reinforce these skills, ensuring that responses become second nature.

Moreover, access to mental health services is essential for addressing both immediate and long-term psychological needs. Crisis counseling, therapy, and support groups should be readily available to those affected by disasters. Integrating mental health services into disaster response plans ensures that psychological care is prioritized alongside physical aid. This comprehensive approach acknowledges the interconnected nature of physical and mental health, promoting holistic recovery.

Community leaders and policymakers also play a crucial role in fostering resilience. Developing policies that prioritize mental health infrastructure, allocating resources for mental health services, and supporting research on trauma and recovery are all steps that can enhance community resilience. Collaboration between governmental agencies, non-profit organizations, and mental health professionals is necessary to create robust support systems tailored to the unique needs of each community.

Summary and Reflections

In this chapter, we explored the different types of catastrophic events and their profound impacts on societies. We looked at natural disasters like earthquakes and hurricanes, man-made catastrophes such as nuclear accidents and terrorist attacks, and the sweeping effects of pandemics. Geopolitical turmoil also plays a significant role in causing societal disruption. By examining these events, we can better understand how quickly society can break down and the importance of preparation for future disruptions.

We also reviewed historical examples of societal collapse, such as the fall of the Roman Empire and the Mayan civilization, to draw lessons that are still relevant today. Environmental changes, social inequality, and political instability were some of the key factors behind these collapses. The psychological toll of disasters is another critical aspect, affecting mental health long after the event has passed. Building community resilience through education, mental health support, and preparedness training helps mitigate these adverse effects. Learning from both history and modern crises enables us to take proactive measures to strengthen our societal defenses.

Reference List

Everything Everywhere All at Once: Wars, Climate Change, Natural Disasters, Coups, and Economic Collapse > Air University (AU) > Journal of Indo-Pacific

Affairs Article Display . (n.d.). Www.airuniversity.af.edu. https://www.airuniversity.af.edu/JIPA/Display/Article/3768335/everything-everywhere-all-at-once-wars-climate-change-natural-disasters-coups-a/

Kemp, L. (2019, February 18). *Are We on the Road to Civilisation collapse?* Bbc.com; BBC Future. https://www.bbc.com/future/article/20190218-are-we-on-the-road-to-civilisation-collapse

Makwana, N. (2019, October 31). *Disaster and Its Impact on Mental health: a Narrative Review* . Journal of Family Medicine and Primary Care. https://doi.org/10.4103/jfmpc.jfmpc_893_19

Meissner, B. (2015). *Types of Disasters   SAMHSA - Substance Abuse and Mental Health Services Administration* . Samhsa.gov. https://www.samhsa.gov/find-help/disaster-distress-helpline/disaster-types

Morganstein, J. (2019, November). *Climate Change and Mental Health* . Psychiatry.org. https://www.psychiatry.org/patients-families/climate-change-and-mental-health-connections/affects-on-mental-health

Societal collapse | City Vision University . (n.d.). Library.cityvision.edu. Retrieved July 29, 2024, from https://library.cityvision.edu/societal-collapse

Chapter Three

Creating a Detailed Survival Plan

Creating a detailed survival plan involves more than just gathering supplies; it requires a thorough understanding of the needs and potential vulnerabilities of each family member. By considering factors such as dietary requirements, medical necessities, and emotional well-being, you can develop a plan that is both comprehensive and adaptable. This chapter will guide you through assessing personal and family needs to ensure that everyone is prepared for any situation that may arise. From evaluating basic essentials like food, water, and shelter, to identifying specific health conditions and dietary restrictions, you'll learn how to tailor your survival strategy to fit your family's unique circumstances.

In addition, this chapter will explore the importance of conducting risk assessments tailored to various emergency scenarios such as natural disasters, economic collapse, or societal breakdown. We'll discuss how to evaluate the likelihood of these events occurring in your region and their potential impact on your household. You'll also discover how to identify individual vulnerabilities within your family unit and assign roles based on strengths and capabilities. Finally, we'll address the psychological impacts of disasters and offer strategies for providing emotional support and creating coping mechanisms. With these insights, you will be well-equipped to formulate a robust and flexible survival plan.

Assessing Personal and Family Needs

Survival planning involves understanding and addressing the specific requirements of individuals and families. This starts with a thorough evaluation of basic needs, such as food, water, shelter, and medical supplies for each family member.

To evaluate these needs, start by determining the necessary amount of food each person will require. Consider factors like age, activity level, and metabolic rate. For example, children and elderly adults may have different caloric needs compared to active adults. It's crucial to stock a variety of non-perishable foods that can cater to everyone's dietary preferences while also ensuring sufficient nutrient intake.

Water is another critical resource. Each person typically needs about one gallon of water per day for drinking and sanitation purposes. In extreme conditions or during high physical activity, this amount may need to be increased. Storing water securely and rotating your supply regularly is vital to prevent contamination and ensure freshness.

Shelter needs vary based on climate, available resources, and personal preferences. In colder climates, having insulated and weatherproof shelters is essential. Conversely, in warmer regions, ventilation and sun protection are more critical. Consider whether your existing home can serve as a shelter or if you need an alternative location, such as a pre-constructed safe house or an emergency tent.

Medical supplies should be tailored to each individual's health requirements. Begin with a well-stocked first aid kit that includes bandages, antiseptics, pain relievers, and necessary prescription medications. Take into account any chronic illnesses or conditions that require specialized equipment or medication. Regularly check expiration dates and adjust the inventory as health conditions change.

Identifying individual dietary restrictions and allergies is another vital step. Food allergies can be life-threatening, so it's crucial to avoid stocking items that could cause adverse reactions. Create a list of acceptable foods for each family member and ensure these items are always included in your storage plan. This reduces the risk of accidental consumption of allergens during stressful situations when attention to detail might slip.

Conducting risk assessments for various emergency situations helps in anticipating possible threats and preparing accordingly. Different scenarios, such as natural disasters, economic collapse, or societal breakdown, present unique challenges. Evaluate the likelihood of each event occurring in your region and its potential impact on your household. For instance, living in an earthquake-prone area requires securing heavy furniture and storing emergency supplies in easily accessible locations.

Risk assessments should also include identifying vulnerabilities within the family unit. This means recognizing who might need additional assistance, such as young children, elderly family members, or those with disabilities. Assign specific roles and responsibilities that play to each person's strengths. For example, someone with medical training can be in charge of healthcare provisions, while someone physically strong can handle manual labor tasks.

Recognizing the psychological impact of disasters is often overlooked but equally important. Disasters can cause significant emotional distress, leading to anxiety, depression, or post-traumatic stress disorder (PTSD). Understanding how different individuals may react helps in creating effective coping mechanisms. Children, for instance, might need extra reassurance and stability, while adults might benefit from structured routines and clear communication channels.

Planning for emotional support within the family unit involves creating a safe environment where everyone feels heard and supported. Establish regular family meetings to discuss concerns and strategies openly. Engage in activities that promote mental well-being, such as mindfulness exercises, physical activity, or hobbies that provide relaxation and enjoyment.

Creating coping mechanisms for stressful situations is another key aspect. These can range from practical strategies like deep breathing exercises to more structured approaches like counseling sessions. Make use of community resources or online support groups to connect with others facing similar challenges. Building a network of mutual support can alleviate feelings of isolation and enhance resilience.

Developing Emergency Plans for Different Scenarios

Anticipating and preparing for a variety of potential emergency situations is essential for effective survival planning. By creating response plans for different scenarios, you can ensure that you are ready to handle any situation that may arise. This section provides guidelines on how to prepare for natural disasters, pandemics, economic collapse, and other emergencies.

First, it's crucial to create detailed response plans for various types of emergencies. Natural disasters such as earthquakes, hurricanes, floods, and tornadoes require specific actions to ensure safety. For instance, if you live in an area prone to hurricanes, your plan should include securing your home, knowing evacuation routes, and having a supply kit ready. In the case of pandemics, ensuring access to medical supplies, following public health guidelines, and practicing good hygiene become paramount. An economic collapse might necessitate strategic financial planning, stockpiling essential goods, and developing skills for self-sufficiency.

Establishing protocols for evacuating in different situations is another critical component of a comprehensive survival plan. Identify the types of emergencies that might require evacuation, such as wildfires, chemical spills, or rising floodwaters. Determine safe locations where you can seek refuge, whether they are local shelters, distant relatives, or designated community centers. Make sure every family member knows these protocols and what their roles are during an evacuation.

Mapping out primary and alternate evacuation routes is a practical step that can save lives during an emergency. Start by identifying the safest and most efficient routes to get from your home or workplace to your pre-determined safe location. Ensure that you have multiple options in case one route becomes impassable. Use maps and GPS devices to familiarize yourself with these routes, and practice driving or walking them to reduce panic and confusion during an actual emergency. Keeping these maps in easily accessible places, both digital and physical copies, will also be beneficial.

Implementing communication drills and practice sessions is vital to ensure all members of your household know what to do and whom to contact during an emergency. Develop a communication plan that includes a list of emergency contacts like family members, neighbors, local authorities, and medical professionals. Assign a person in charge of disseminating information to avoid confusion. Schedule regular drills where you practice the communication plan, testing different scenarios to identify any weaknesses or areas for improvement.

In preparation for natural disasters, conducting risk analysis is key. Evaluate the likelihood of various natural events in your area and prioritize your preparations based on these risks. For example, if you live in a region known for frequent earthquakes, invest in securing heavy furniture, creating a stash of emergency supplies, and learning basic first aid. This method ensures that your efforts and resources are focused where they are most needed.

Pandemic preparedness involves not only stockpiling medical supplies but also understanding and practicing disease prevention measures. This includes regular handwashing, using personal protective equipment (PPE) when necessary, and keeping up-to-date with vaccinations. Information programs and webinars, such as those offered by CDC's Clinician Outreach and Communication Activity (COCA), can provide invaluable insights (CDC, 2018).

Economic collapse scenarios demand readiness in terms of financial stability and resource management. This could mean diversifying income streams, reducing debt, and investing in tangible assets like food, water, and tools. Learn skills such as gardening, carpentry, or basic mechanics to help your community and barter services if currency becomes unstable. Establishing a network of trusted individuals for mutual support can increase resilience.

For effective evacuation planning, consider the unique needs of each family member, including pets. Pack go-bags containing essentials like medications, identification, cash, water, non-perishable food, and personal hygiene items. Customize these bags according to specific requirements, such as baby formula for infants or special dietary foods for those with allergies.

Communication strategies during emergencies also benefit from modern technology. Explore the use of apps and services that provide real-time alerts and enable group messaging. Social media platforms, radio broadcasts, and emergency apps like the Red Cross Emergency App offer timely updates and connection points. However, in case of infrastructure failure, having backup methods such as walkie-talkies, CB radios, or even pre-agreed signals can be invaluable.

It's important to run these communication drills periodically to reinforce everyone's knowledge and readiness. Simulate different emergency conditions where traditional communication lines might be cut off. Adapt your strategies based on feedback from these exercises, and remain flexible to incorporate new technologies and methods as they become available.

Anticipating a range of emergencies allows you to develop flexible plans that can be adapted as situations change. Regularly review and update your emergency plans to account for new risks or changes in your living situation or environment. Knowledge and preparation empower you to respond effectively, minimize risks, and ensure the safety of you and your loved ones.

Establishing Communication Protocols

Developing clear communication strategies to maintain connectivity during emergencies is crucial for survival. Effective communication ensures that all members of a group stay informed, coordinated, and can react promptly to changing situations. This section will delve into the necessary steps to create a robust communication plan for emergencies.

First and foremost, it is essential to outline the types of communication tools needed for emergencies. Different scenarios may require various tools, and having a diverse set of options increases the chances of maintaining connectivity. Traditional mobile phones are often the primary means of communication; however, they are unreliable in cases where cellular networks fail due to heavy usage or infrastructure damage. Therefore, it is advisable to invest in alternative communication devices such as two-way radios, satellite phones, and even ham radios which do not depend on local cell towers and can reach long distances. Two-way radios are particularly useful for short-range communication within a specific area, while satellite phones provide a more reliable option for long-distance communication when other networks are down. For those with the know-how, ham radios offer a versatile option capable of both short and long-range communication.

In addition to equipping oneself with various communication tools, it is equally important to compile comprehensive contact lists for emergency communication. These lists should include immediate family members, close friends, neighbors, local emergency services, and relevant authorities. A well-organized contact list ensures that everyone knows who to reach out to during different stages of an emergency. It's also beneficial to include contacts for utilities such as gas, electricity, and water suppliers, as well as medical professionals like doctors and veterinarians if pets are part of the household. Keeping this list accessible is vital; storing it in both digital form (in mobile phones and computers) and physical printouts ensures it remains available even if electronic devices fail.

Implementing coded language and signals for secure communication adds another layer of reliability and security to your emergency communication strategy. During crises, preventing the leakage of sensitive information is crucial. Coded language and signals can help achieve this by disguising the nature of messages from potential eavesdroppers. Simple codes can be devised for common instructions or locations. For instance, phrases like "Code Blue" could signify an immediate need for assistance, while "Base Alpha" might refer to a pre-determined safe location. It's important to keep the codes straightforward yet unique enough so that they can't be easily deciphered by outsiders. Everyone involved must be aware of these codes and understand their meanings to ensure smooth and efficient communication.

Moreover, practicing communication drills with code words and signals reinforces their use and effectiveness. Regular practice allows individuals to familiarize themselves with the communication protocols and adjust them as needed based on the specifics of the emergency scenario. These drills should simulate real-life situations to test and refine your plan. For example, families can conduct monthly drills where they pretend to encounter different emergencies, such as natural disasters or sudden evacuations, during which they communicate solely through predetermined codes and alternative methods. Incorporating feedback from these drills helps improve the overall communication plan and ensures that everyone remains prepared.

Let's consider an example to illustrate the necessity of a well-rounded communication strategy. Imagine a scenario where a family is forced to evacuate due to a rapidly approaching wildfire. Having multiple communication tools ensures they stay connected even if one method fails. The father communicates with distant relatives via a satellite phone, while the mother coordinates with nearby neighbors using a two-way radio. Meanwhile, their son tunes into a ham radio for updates on the fire's progress. Their comprehensive contact list allows them to quickly alert and check on essential contacts. They use coded language to inform each other about their status without revealing sensitive information over potentially unsecured channels. Because they have practiced these drills regularly, they execute their plan smoothly despite the stressful situation.

Communication drills should also involve the use of different communication tools, ensuring that every family member is comfortable with operating equipment like two-way radios and satellite phones. Mock scenarios can be created to hone skills in switching between devices when one becomes unusable. For instance, if cellular networks are down, drills can practice transitioning to satellite phones seamlessly. This practical experience is invaluable, as it builds confidence and reduces panic during actual emergencies.

Lastly, integrating modern technology into your communication plan can greatly enhance its effectiveness. Apps designed for emergency communication, like Zello, turn smartphones into walkie-talkies, providing a quick way to connect with group members. Emergency alert apps can send notifications about nearby dangers, while GPS tracking apps help monitor everyone's location in real-time. However, it's critical to remember that these technologies depend on internet access, which may be unreliable during certain emergencies. Therefore, they should complement rather than replace traditional communication tools.

Final Insights

In this chapter, we focused on the importance of creating a survival strategy that is comprehensive and adaptable to various situations. By thoroughly evaluating personal and family needs, such as food, water, shelter, and medical supplies, we laid the foundation for an effective plan. We also highlighted the necessity of understanding dietary restrictions, conducting risk assessments, and recognizing psychological impacts to ensure the well-being of all family members. This meticulous approach helps prepare us for a wide range of emergencies, from natural disasters to societal breakdowns.

We also explored the development of emergency plans tailored to different scenarios. Building detailed response plans, establishing evacuation protocols, and practicing communication drills are critical steps in maintaining readiness. Being equipped with the right tools and having a clear understanding of each family member's role during emergencies enhances our ability to respond effectively. Regularly reviewing and updating these strategies ensures they remain relevant and robust. Through proactive planning and preparation, we can face unforeseen challenges with confidence and resilience, safeguarding ourselves and our loved ones.

Reference List

CDC. (2018). *Emergency Preparedness and Response | CDC* . Cdc.gov. https://emergency.cdc.gov/

Committee on Post-Disaster Recovery of a Community's Public Health, Medical, and Social Services, Board on Health Sciences Policy, & Institute of Medicine. (2015, September 10). *Social Services* . Nih.gov; National Academies Press (US). https://www.ncbi.nlm.nih.gov/books/NBK316542/

Ellery, J. (2012, May 2). *Radio Communication Procedure for Security* . Security Solutions Media. https://www.securitysolutionsmedia.com/2012/05/02/radio-communication-for-security/

Emergency Preparedness and Response | Occupational Safety and Health Administration . (n.d.). Www.osha.gov. https://www.osha.gov/emergency-preparedness

Meissner, B. (2023, June 9). *Warning Signs and Risk Factors* . Www.samhsa.gov. https://www.samhsa.gov/find-help/disaster-distress-helpline/warning-signs-risk-factors

Savoia, E., Lin, L., & Viswanath, K. (2013, September). *Communications in Public Health Emergency Preparedness: A Systematic Review of the Literature* . Biosecurity and Bioterrorism: Biodefense Strategy, Practice, and Science. https://doi.org/10.1089/bsp.2013.0038

Chapter Four

Essential Supplies for Survival

Gathering essential supplies for survival is a critical aspect of being prepared for emergencies. Whether facing natural disasters, economic downturns, or societal upheavals, having the right resources on hand can make all the difference in ensuring your and your family's well-being. In times of crisis, instant access to these vital supplies mitigates panic and allows for more focused and effective actions to safeguard health and safety.

In this chapter, you will delve into the exhaustive list of necessary items that should be included in a well-prepared survival kit. From first-aid essentials to non-perishable foods, each category is thoroughly covered, offering not only what to include but also how to organize and manage these supplies efficiently. Practical advice on proper storage techniques, rotation of perishable goods, and maintenance of medicinal inventories are detailed to help you stay prepared. By the end of this chapter, you will have a clear understanding of what constitutes a comprehensive survival kit and how to maintain it to ensure readiness in any emergency scenario.

First-aid and Medical Supplies

When considering survival scenarios, having a comprehensive understanding of first-aid and medical supplies is paramount. In any crisis, from natural disasters to economic collapse, the immediate availability and proper management of these supplies can mean the difference between life and death.

One of the foundational steps in preparedness is the selection of appropriate first-aid kits. First-aid kits come in various types tailored for different needs and situations. For example, basic household first-aid kits are designed for treating minor injuries like cuts, burns, and abrasions. These typically include bandages, antiseptics, gauze pads, adhesive tape, and pain relievers. However, for more extreme conditions, such as wilderness survival or long-term economic disruption, a more comprehensive kit is necessary. Such kits should include items like splints, tourniquets, hemostatic agents (for severe bleeding), and tools for stitching wounds (American Red Cross, 2023).

In addition to these basic components, consider personalizing your first-aid kit based on specific health concerns. This might include adding prescription medications, specific medical devices, or allergy treatments that cater to individual family members' needs. When assembling or purchasing a kit, ensure it includes not only the essentials but also any special items recommended by healthcare providers.

It's equally important to organize these supplies efficiently for ease of access. In an emergency, quick response is crucial, and rummaging through a disorganized kit wastes precious time. A well-organized first-aid kit should have clear labels and compartments, making it easy to locate items swiftly. Items should be grouped logically—wound care supplies together, medication in another section, and tools like tweezers and scissors in their designated place. Regularly check the kit for expired items and replace them to ensure everything is ready when needed (Fuerst, 2019).

Beyond the physical contents of a first-aid kit, medical training plays a critical role in emergency preparedness. Having a first-aid kit is useless if you don't know how to use it properly. Basic medical training, such as CPR and the Heimlich maneuver, can be life-saving skills. Certification courses offered by organizations like the American Red Cross or the American Heart Association provide practical knowledge and the confidence needed to administer aid effectively. Individuals trained in first aid are equipped not only with theoretical knowledge but also with hands-on skills that can stabilize a person until professional help arrives.

Medicinal supplies and prescription management are other vital components of survival planning. Stockpiling essential medicines involves maintaining a supply of over-the-counter drugs like pain relievers, anti-inflammatory medications, antihistamines, and antidiarrheals. For those with chronic conditions, managing prescriptions becomes even more crucial. It's advisable to have at least a three-month supply of prescription medications, noting expiration dates and ensuring that they are stored under conditions that maintain their efficacy. Rotating your stockpile regularly can help keep medications from expiring before use.

Moreover, knowing alternative uses for common medications can extend their utility in survival scenarios. For instance, aspirin, commonly used for pain and fever, can also serve as an anti-inflammatory agent, while antihistamines can treat allergic reactions and alleviate symptoms of insect bites or stings.

For practical implementation, let's break down how to set up an effective, accessible first-aid station within your home. Choose a location that is both secure and easily reachable. The kitchen, as a central hub of activity, often serves as a good spot, though it's important to avoid bathrooms due to their high humidity levels, which can degrade medical supplies more quickly. If space permits, install shelves or designated storage units where kits can be neatly arranged. Each item or group of items should have a clearly marked label for quick identification, and instructions for use should be easily visible or included within the kit. Maintaining a checklist of contents can help keep track of what needs replenishing.

As part of organizing your first-aid resources, educate all family members about the locations of these supplies and how to use them. In many cases, the person needing aid may be the one who usually administers it; thus, training every household member ensures that everyone can assist if required. Moreover, periodic drills can reinforce this knowledge, making everyone more adept at handling real emergencies calmly and efficiently.

Non-Perishable Food Items

Non-perishable food items play a crucial role in maintaining sustenance during crises. When natural disasters, economic downturns, or other emergencies disrupt regular food supply chains, having a well-stocked pantry of non-perishable foods can make a significant difference. These foods offer the advantage of long shelf life, stability without refrigeration, and straightforward preparation methods, ensuring individuals have access to nutrition when it's needed most.

Selection and Storage of Non-Perishables

Choosing the right non-perishable food items is foundational to emergency preparedness. A variety of options should be considered, including canned goods, dried foods, and ready-to-eat meals (MREs). Canned fruits, vegetables, beans, meats, fish, and soups are excellent choices as they require no refrigeration and minimal preparation. Dry items such as rice, pasta, oats, and powdered milk also fall into this category but will need water for preparation, which should be factored into your planning.

Proper storage of these items is paramount. To maximize their lifespan, store non-perishable foods in cool, dry places away from direct sunlight. Use sealed containers to protect against pests and moisture. Additionally, labeling each item with its purchase date helps track what needs to be used first, ensuring older items are consumed before they spoil. Consider investing in shelves dedicated to emergency food supplies, keeping the most frequently used items easily accessible while less perishable items can be stored further back.

Food Preparation Methods

In many crisis scenarios, you might not have access to traditional cooking facilities such as stoves or ovens. Therefore, knowing how to prepare non-perishable food using alternative methods is essential. MREs and canned goods often come ready to eat and can be consumed cold if necessary. For foods requiring heat, consider using portable stoves, grills, or even a fireplace if indoors. In cases where open flames are unsafe or impractical, chemically heated meal packs provide an excellent alternative, using a chemical reaction to produce heat when mixed with water.

For dried foods like rice or oats, pre-packaged serving sizes in airtight containers can simplify preparation. Instant varieties of these foods require only boiling water, which can be heated using camping stoves or solar cookers if traditional means are unavailable. It's also wise to keep a manual can opener as electric ones won't work during power outages.

Rationing and Meal Planning

Effective rationing and meal planning are critical to making your food supplies last throughout the duration of an emergency. Start by determining the caloric needs of each individual in your household, taking into account age, health status, and activity levels. Create a daily meal plan that meets these nutritional requirements while maximizing resource efficiency.

One strategy is to divide food supplies into daily rations. Label meals by date and include notes on water and utensil needs, forcing you to think through the entire process of preparation and consumption. This method ensures organized and efficient use of your resources, preventing waste and over-consumption.

Remember to incorporate high-energy foods that require minimal preparation, such as peanut butter, dried fruits, nuts, and granola bars. These can serve as convenient snacks and help maintain energy levels between meals, contributing to better overall resource management.

Rotating food supplies is another crucial aspect of effective stockpile management. Regularly check the expiration dates of your stored items and integrate them into your routine meal plans to ensure nothing goes to waste. As new supplies are purchased, place them at the back of the storage area, moving older items to the front to be used first. This "first in, first out" approach helps maintain the freshness and usability of your food stockpile, reducing the risk of spoilage.

Rotating Food Supplies

To prevent spoilage and maintain freshness, it's important to regularly rotate your food supplies. This practice not only ensures that you always have viable food options available but also keeps your inventory manageable and up-to-date. Begin by categorizing your stored foods based on their expiration dates. Frequently check these dates and make it a habit to consume items nearing their end of life first. Incorporate these into your daily meals to avoid waste.

When adding new items to your stockpile, place them behind the older items. This systematic rotation ensures that the oldest products are used first, thus minimizing the risk of spoilage. Additionally, purchasing smaller quantities more frequently rather than bulk buying all at once can help maintain a fresher stock of non-perishable food items.

Maintaining proper records also aids in managing your food supplies effectively. Keeping an inventory list with purchase and expiration dates allows you to monitor what needs to be consumed soon and what can be stored longer. By doing so, you can plan your meals accordingly and reduce the likelihood of any food going bad unnoticed.

Conclusion

Water Storage Solutions

Water is one of the most crucial resources when it comes to survival preparedness. Ensuring an adequate and safe supply of water can be the difference between life and death in emergency situations. This section aims to educate readers on the critical aspects of water storage solutions, focusing on the types of water containers, purification methods, water usage management, and proper labeling techniques.

Types of Water Containers

When planning for emergency water storage, choosing the right type of container is vital. Different containers offer various benefits and limitations based on your specific needs and circumstances. One of the most recommended options is food-grade plastic containers, which are specifically designed to store potable water without leaching harmful chemicals. These can often be found in surplus or camping supply stores.

For smaller quantities, commercially bottled water is the safest and most reliable option. These bottles are sealed and treated to maintain water quality for extended periods. Larger containers, such as 5-gallon jugs with spigots, are also convenient for dispensing water without contamination. For those needing even larger capacities, 55-gallon drums are an excellent choice but require more space and handling care due to their size and weight.

Metal containers, like stainless steel, are durable and do not degrade over time. However, they are generally heavier and can be more expensive. Glass containers are another option, but they are fragile and need careful handling and storage to avoid breakage.

It's crucial to avoid containers that have previously held toxic materials. Even after thorough cleaning, residues can persist and contaminate the stored water, making it unsafe to drink. Always use containers with tight-fitting lids that can be securely closed to prevent contamination.

Purification Methods

No matter how rigorous your initial water collection process, it's essential to employ purification methods to maintain potability and safety. Boiling water is one of the simplest and most effective ways to kill pathogens. Bringing water to a rolling boil for at least one minute will eliminate most bacteria, viruses, and parasites.

Chemical disinfection is another viable method. Household chlorine bleach can be used if it contains 5-9% sodium hypochlorite. Add 8 drops of bleach per gallon of water, stir well, and let it sit for at least 30 minutes before drinking. The water should have a slight chlorine odor; if not, repeat the process.

Portable water filters, such as those used by campers and hikers, can remove bacteria, protozoa, and other impurities. Filters with activated carbon elements are particularly useful as they can also improve the taste and odor of the water. Some advanced filters even include UV light purification, providing an additional layer of protection against viruses.

Solar water disinfection (SODIS) is a method where you fill transparent plastic bottles with water and expose them to full sunlight for at least six hours. The UV rays from the sun kill most microorganisms, making the water safer to drink. While this method is cost-effective, it requires clear skies and cannot treat large volumes of water efficiently.

Water Usage Management

In survival scenarios, efficient water usage is crucial to ensure that your supplies last as long as possible. First and foremost, rationing water appropriately can help manage limited resources. During emergencies, the general guideline is to store at least one gallon of water per person per day for drinking and sanitation purposes. If possible, aim to store a two-week supply.

Conserving water is equally important. Use water sparingly for hygiene activities such as brushing teeth or washing hands. Opt for waterless hygiene products when available. In cooking, consider meals that require minimal water or use the same water for multiple tasks, such as boiling vegetables and then using that water for soups.

Implementing a schedule for water use can also be beneficial. Allocate specific amounts of water for different times of the day and adhere strictly to this plan. This helps in monitoring your consumption and prevents the depletion of your reserves prematurely.

Labeling Water Containers

Proper labeling of water containers is an often overlooked but vital part of water storage. Label each container clearly as "drinking water" and include the date when the water was stored. This practice ensures that you can keep track of when water needs to be rotated or replaced. Stored water should be replaced every six months to maintain its freshness and safety.

Additionally, include purification instructions on the labels. This can be crucial during stressful situations when you might forget the necessary steps to make the water potable. Detailed labeling helps everyone involved follow the correct procedures and minimizes the risk of consuming contaminated water.

Summary and Reflections

Throughout this chapter, we explored the essential components and management of critical supplies needed for survival. From selecting and personalizing first-aid kits to stockpiling and effectively rotating non-perishable foods, each aspect plays a crucial role in emergency preparedness. We delved into the importance of organizing medical supplies for quick access, the value of basic medical training, and how to maintain a sufficient stock of prescription medications. Moreover, understanding the various types of non-perishable foods, proper storage techniques, and alternative preparation methods ensures that sustenance is available even when conventional means are disrupted.

Water storage solutions were another vital component discussed, highlighting the importance of choosing appropriate containers, utilizing effective purification methods, and managing water usage wisely. Proper labeling and regular rotation of supplies ensure they remain safe and usable. By implementing these strategies, you can create a well-rounded and efficient plan for survival during emergencies. The knowledge and practices outlined in this chapter provide a solid foundation for being better prepared, ensuring that you and your loved ones have the resources needed to face unforeseen challenges with confidence.

Reference List

American Red Cross. (2023). *Make a First Aid Kit* . American Red Cross. https://www.redcross.org/get-help/how-to-prepare-for-emergencies/anatomy-of-a-first-aid-kit.html

Creating & storing an emergency water supply . (2021, January 26). Centers for Disease Control and Prevention. https://www.cdc.gov/healthywater/emergency/creating-storing-emergency-water-supply.html

Food | Ready.gov . (2019). Ready.gov. https://www.ready.gov/food

Fuerst, R. (2019, September 23). *First Aid Kits - 33 Essentials to Prepare for Emergencies* . EMedicineHealth; eMedicineHealth. https://www.emedicinehealth.com/first_aid_kits/article_em.htm

Preparing an Emergency Food Supply, Short Term Food Storage | Food Preservation | Food | Extension | UGA FACS . (n.d.). Www.fcs.uga.edu. https://www.fcs.uga.edu/extension/preparing-an-emergency-food-supply-short-term-food-storage

dyaniwood. (2017, December 8). *Home Water Storage for an Emergency* . Utah Department of Environmental Quality. https://deq.utah.gov/drinking-water/emergency-water-storage

Chapter Five

Building a Sustainable Food Supply

Building a sustainable food supply post-disaster is essential for long-term survival and resilience. Home gardening and farming stand as powerful tools in achieving this goal, offering numerous benefits that can greatly enhance food security. The ability to grow your own food provides not only immediate nutritional value but also a means to sustain oneself when conventional food systems fail. Understanding key practices such as the optimal timing for planting, constructing raised beds, and implementing composting can significantly boost the productivity and reliability of home gardens.

This chapter will guide you through various strategies to maintain a continuous and reliable food source after a disaster. You'll learn about the importance of aligning crop planting with seasonal changes to ensure healthy growth and consistent harvests. The advantages of constructing raised beds, including better soil management and efficient space utilization, will be explored. Additionally, the chapter will delve into composting practices that enhance soil fertility and reduce waste. By integrating these methods, you'll be well-equipped to create a sustainable home garden that contributes to long-term food security.

Home Gardening and Farming

Exploring the importance of home gardening and farming in cultivating a sustainable food source reveals a multitude of benefits that can enhance long-term food security, especially post-disaster. Understanding some foundational practices can significantly contribute to the success of home gardens, making them viable sources of nutrition.

One primary aspect is understanding the optimal timing for planting different crops in alignment with seasonal changes. Plants have specific requirements depending not only on their species but also on local climate conditions. For example, leafy greens like lettuce and spinach thrive in cooler temperatures and should be planted in early spring or late summer. Conversely, warm-season crops such as tomatoes, peppers, and melons need the warmer weather of late spring to early summer to flourish. Properly timed planting ensures that crops get the ideal conditions they need to grow robustly and yield effectively. Additionally, it helps in staggering harvest times, so there is a continuous supply of fresh produce rather than a glut followed by a dry spell.

Constructing raised beds can greatly improve garden efficiency and soil health. Raised beds are essentially elevated sections of soil encased within a· frame, providing benefits such as better drainage, easier access for planting and harvesting, and concentrated nutrient management. They allow gardeners to control soil quality more precisely, ensuring that plants receive optimal nutrition. Moreover, raised beds can be built in compact areas, maximizing limited space, which is particularly beneficial in urban settings where ground space may be at a premium. Ensuring the soil composition within these beds includes a mix of compost, topsoil, and organic matter promotes healthy plant growth and can lead to higher yields.

Implementing composting practices is another crucial element in creating a sustainable home garden. Composting involves the breakdown of organic materials like kitchen scraps and yard waste into rich, fertile humus that enhances soil structure and fertility. This practice not only reduces household waste—which would otherwise end up in landfills—but also returns valuable nutrients to the soil, fostering healthier plants. A well-maintained compost pile includes a balanced ratio of green (nitrogen-rich) and brown (carbon-rich) materials, aerated often to support decomposition. The resulting compost can be used to enrich garden beds, potting mixes, and even as mulch around plants.

The integration of these practices aligns closely with the concept of home gardening as fundamental infrastructure in sustainable societies. As noted by Santos et al. (2022), private backyards and home gardens play a significant role in supplementing food systems, particularly in emergency scenarios. These gardens provide essential ecosystem services, including biodiversity conservation and increased resilience against disruptions caused by natural disasters or economic instabilities. The spatial importance of these small plots should not be underestimated; they contribute significantly to local ecosystems and community wellbeing.

Home gardens offer diverse social, economic, and environmental benefits. Growing one's own food can provide a direct and personal connection to nature, enhancing physical activity and mental wellbeing. Engaging in gardening activities can be both therapeutic and educational, offering opportunities to learn about sustainable practices. It fosters a deeper appreciation of food production processes, leading to more informed choices about consumption and diet.

Moreover, home gardening has been associated with improved nutrition and food quality. Unlike commercial agriculture, which often focuses on appearance and shelf-life, home gardens emphasize the growth of nutrient-dense, flavorful produce. Allen (2021) highlights that home-grown food tends to taste better and can be more nutritious due to the ability to manage soil health closely. Growers can amend their soil with organic compost, minerals, and other nutrients, encouraging robust microbial activity essential for healthy plant development.

Gardening also contributes positively to environmental health. By reducing reliance on industrial agriculture, which accounts for a substantial portion of global carbon emissions, home gardens help mitigate climate impact. The reduction in transportation needs for produce—grown and consumed locally—further decreases fossil fuel use. Additionally, home gardens provide habitats for beneficial insects and wildlife, promoting biodiversity and ecological balance.

Preserving and Storing Food

In the aftermath of a disaster, securing a long-term food supply becomes paramount. One of the most critical strategies to achieve this is through proper food preservation and storage methods. These techniques ensure that food remains safe to consume over extended periods, reducing waste and providing nutritional sustenance when fresh supplies are unavailable. Let's delve into some effective methods for preserving and storing food in ways that can significantly extend its shelf life.

Canning and jarring are two of the most versatile methods for storing food long-term. This process involves placing foods in jars or cans and heating them to a temperature that destroys microorganisms and inactivates enzymes that can cause spoilage. The heat also drives air out of the jar, creating a vacuum seal as it cools, which prevents new bacteria from entering. There are two main types of canning: water bath canning and pressure canning. Water bath canning is suitable for high-acid foods like fruits, pickles, and tomatoes, while pressure canning is necessary for low-acid foods such as meats, vegetables, and soups to ensure safety from botulism (*Principles for Food Preservation - the Homesteading RD*, 2023). Both methods require specific equipment, such as canners, jars, lids, and rings, as well as adherence to tested recipes to ensure safety and effectiveness.

Building and utilizing a root cellar is an ancient yet highly effective method for storing root vegetables, fruits, and other produce. Root cellars take advantage of the natural cooling, insulating, and humidifying properties of the earth to create an environment that keeps produce fresh for months. To construct a basic root cellar, you can dig a pit in a shaded area and line it with shelves or bins for storage. Modern adaptations include using basements or specially designed containers that mimic the conditions of traditional root cellars. The key is maintaining a consistent, cool temperature and high humidity level while ensuring good ventilation to prevent mold growth. Properly prepared and maintained root cellars can be invaluable in extending the availability of homegrown or locally sourced produce throughout the colder months (*Preserving Your Harvest: Methods and Techniques for Long-Term Food Storage*, n.d.).

Vacuum sealing is another excellent method for prolonging the shelf life of food items by removing air, one of the primary causes of spoilage. This technique involves placing food in special plastic bags and using a vacuum sealer to extract all the air before sealing the bag tightly. By eliminating oxygen, vacuum sealing significantly slows down the process of oxidation, which can lead to rancidity and spoilage. It also inhibits the growth of aerobic bacteria and fungi. Vacuum-sealed food can be stored in the pantry, refrigerator, or freezer, depending on the type of food and desired shelf life. This method works particularly well for dry goods like grains, nuts, and pasta, as well as for meats and cheeses (*Principles for Food Preservation - the Homesteading RD*, 2023).

Dehydration is one of the oldest methods of food preservation, dating back thousands of years. It involves removing moisture from food, which inhibits the growth of bacteria, yeast, and molds. Dehydrating can be done using a food dehydrator, an oven set at a low temperature, or even air-drying in certain climates. This process is particularly effective for preserving fruits, vegetables, and meats. To dehydrate food properly, it should be uniformly sliced or chopped to ensure even drying, then placed in the dehydrator or oven until all moisture has evaporated. The dried food should be stored in airtight containers in a cool, dark place to maintain its quality and prevent reabsorption of moisture. Dehydrated foods are lightweight and compact, making them ideal for emergency food supplies and easy to transport or store (*Principles for Food Preservation - the Homesteading RD*, 2023).

Each of these methods offers unique advantages and can be adapted to suit different needs and resources. Canning and jarring provide a way to store a wide variety of foods at room temperature, making them readily accessible during emergencies. Root cellaring utilizes natural resources and requires minimal energy inputs, offering a sustainable solution for storing seasonal produce without refrigeration. Vacuum sealing extends the shelf life of both dry and perishable goods, protecting them from spoilage and contamination. Dehydration reduces the weight and volume of foods, making them easier to store and carry.

Implementing these preservation techniques not only ensures a stable food supply post-disaster but also contributes to overall food security by reducing dependence on commercial food systems. In times of crisis, having a well-preserved stockpile of food can make a significant difference in maintaining health and morale. By mastering these methods, individuals can take control of their food supply, enhancing their resilience and preparedness for any situation.

Foraging, Hunting, and Fishing Techniques

Foraging, hunting, and fishing serve as vital supplementary food sources in survival scenarios. When disaster strikes and conventional food supplies dwindle, these skills become essential for sustaining a long-term food supply. Understanding how to identify edible wild plants and mushrooms, hunt wild game, fish in various aquatic environments, and utilize trapping techniques can significantly enhance your self-sufficiency and resilience.

Learning to identify edible wild plants and mushrooms is a critical skill. Foraging provides access to a variety of nutritious foods that might be unavailable otherwise. Wild edibles, such as dandelions, nettles, and berries, grow in many regions and can be harvested with minimal tools. It's crucial to learn the characteristics of these plants to avoid confusion with poisonous species. For instance, wild carrot looks very similar to the lethal poison hemlock (House, n.d.). A good field guide or instruction from an experienced forager can help you make accurate identifications. Taking hands-on classes or guided foraging hikes is highly recommended. This knowledge not only increases your food options but also boosts your confidence in utilizing the natural resources around you.

Hunting methods for wild game provide a sustainable protein source that complements other food acquisition strategies. Small game like rabbits, squirrels, and birds are often more abundant and easier to catch than larger animals like deer or elk. Traps and snares can be efficient tools for capturing small game without expending too much energy. Learning to use a bow or firearm effectively can broaden your hunting capabilities. However, it's important to understand local wildlife behavior and habitat preferences to increase your chances of success. Ethical hunting practices, such as maintaining healthy animal populations and using every part of the animal, ensure sustainability. In survival situations, having basic butchering skills can help you process meat efficiently and avoid waste.

Fishing is another indispensable skill, providing a steady supply of protein-rich food. Mastering angling techniques allows you to fish in different water bodies, from rivers and lakes to oceans and streams. Different environments require different approaches, so understanding the behavior and habitats of various fish species is crucial. Simple tools like fishing lines, hooks, and bait can yield significant results if used correctly. For example, knowing when and where to fish during spawning seasons can increase your catch rates. Additionally, learning to construct makeshift fishing gear from available materials can be a lifesaver when conventional equipment is not accessible. Skills such as cleaning and filleting fish ensure you can prepare and preserve your catch effectively.

Integrating trapping skills into your overall food acquisition strategy enhances your ability to secure diverse food sources. Traps can work continuously while you focus on other survival tasks, making them a valuable tool in resource management. Types of traps range from simple snares to more complex designs like deadfalls. The key is to place traps in high-traffic areas where animals frequently travel. Understanding animal tracks and signs can help you select optimal trap locations. As with hunting, ethical considerations are paramount; using humane traps and checking them regularly reduces unnecessary suffering. Incorporating a variety of traps into your strategy increases the likelihood of a successful catch, ensuring a more balanced and dependable food supply.

Foraging requires identifying safe-to-eat plants and avoiding poisonous ones. Many edible plants are found close to home, including groundcover plants like wild leeks and lamb's quarter. Timing is crucial, as some plants are best harvested during specific seasons. For example, stinging nettles should be collected before they flower, and certain mushrooms, like morels, are typically found in spring (House, n.d.). Keeping a foraging journal helps track seasonal patterns, improving future foraging success.

Hunting demands knowledge of both prey and habitat. Smaller game is often more reliable than larger animals, which may be overhunted in times of crisis. Trapping offers a passive method to collect food, allowing multitasking. Bow and firearm proficiency are valuable, but conserving ammunition is crucial. Dressing and processing game efficiently prevents spoilage and maximizes utility.

Fishing adapts to various settings, providing a consistent protein source. Techniques vary by environment, requiring knowledge of local fish behaviors. Simpler tools may suffice, but improvisation skills are beneficial. Regular maintenance of fishing gear ensures readiness, and knowing multiple preparation methods guards against monotony. Seasonality impacts availability, so awareness of breeding cycles aids planning.

Trapping enriches your strategy by passively securing food. Effective traps work around the clock, maximizing efficiency. Placement in frequented areas increases success rates. Ethics in trapping, such as reducing animal suffering, maintain ecological balance. Diverse trap types, from snares to deadfalls, cater to different animals and situations.

The integration of these skills forms a comprehensive approach to survival food sourcing. Each method supports the others, creating a resilient system. Foraging supplements diet with micronutrients, hunting and trapping offer substantial protein, and fishing provides variety. All skills demand practice and local knowledge, emphasizing continuous learning. By mastering foraging, hunting, fishing, and trapping, you strengthen your survival preparedness, ensuring a sustainable food supply in any scenario.

Final Thoughts

In this chapter, we've explored various strategies for sustaining a long-term food supply in the aftermath of a disaster. From home gardening and farming to preserving and storing food, each method provides unique benefits that can be adapted to different circumstances. Home gardening offers fresh produce and environmental benefits, while proper food preservation techniques ensure that these foods remain safe and nutriticus over extended periods. By mastering practices like canning, vacuum sealing, and using root cellars, you can create a resilient food system that supports your needs during emergencies.

Additionally, we discussed essential skills in foraging, hunting, and fishing that can supplement your food supply when traditional sources are unavailable. Identifying edible wild plants, ethically hunting game, and efficiently catching fish are critical components of self-sufficiency. Integrating these methods creates a diversified approach to food security, reducing reliance on commercial systems and enhancing overall preparedness. These skills not only provide immediate solutions but also build long-term resilience, ensuring you and your loved ones remain well-fed and secure in any scenario.

Reference List

Allen, M. (2021, August). *The 6 environmental and health benefits of growing your own food* . The Garden Continuum. https://www.thegardencontinuum.com/blog/the-6-environmental-and-health-benefits-of-growing-your-own-food

Bedford, L. (2023, May 14). *How to Forage: Feed Yourself With Wild Foods - Survival Mom* . The Survival Mom. https://thesurvivalmom.com/how-to-forage/

House, M. (n.d.). *How to Forage for Food in the Wild: A Beginner's Guide* . Mountain House. Retrieved July 29, 2024, from https://mountainhouse.com/blogs/emergency-prep-survival/foraging-for-food-guide

Principles for Food Preservation - The Homesteading RD . (2023, December 6). Thehomesteadingrd.com. https://thehomesteadingrd.com/principles-for-food-preservation/

Preserving Your Harvest: Methods and Techniques for Long-Term Food Storage . (n.d.). Reagtools.co.uk. Retrieved July 29, 2024, from https://reagtools.co.uk/blogs/news/preserving-your-harvest-methods-and-techniques-for-long-term-food-storage

Santos, M., Moreira, H., Cabral, J. A., Gabriel, R., Teixeira, A., Bastos, R., & Aires, A. (2022, October 21). *Contribution of Home Gardens to Sustainable Development: Perspectives from a Supported Opinion Essay* . International

Journal of Environmental Research and Public Health. https://doi.org/10.3390/ijerph192013715

Chapter Six

Ensuring Access to Clean Water

Ensuring access to clean water is a vital skill in survival situations. Whether you're stranded in the wilderness or preparing for emergency scenarios like natural disasters, understanding how to source, purify, and store water can make all the difference. Water is essential not just for hydration but for maintaining overall health and functionality. Learning the methods to locate natural water sources, purify potentially contaminated water, and store it safely for long-term use are fundamental aspects of preparedness that every survivalist should master.

In this chapter, we will delve into various strategies for finding natural water sources, focusing on key indicators like wildlife behavior and vegetation patterns. We will also explore how to use navigation tools such as maps and compasses to find hidden water bodies. Next, we will cover different techniques for purifying water, including boiling, chemical treatments, and portable filtration systems. Finally, we will discuss the best practices for storing water securely over extended periods, ensuring that your supply remains safe and potable. This comprehensive guide aims to equip you with the knowledge necessary to secure clean water in any survival situation.

Locating natural water sources

Understanding how to find safe and reliable natural water sources is crucial for survival situations. When you're in the wilderness, knowing where to look can mean the difference between life and death.

Identifying key indicators in nature that hint at nearby water sources is a skill everyone should master. Wildlife behavior, for example, can provide valuable clues. Animals need water just as much as humans do, and their habits often lead them to reliable sources. Birds, especially grain-eating species, tend to stay close to water. If you see birds flying low in the evening or early morning, particularly in arid regions, follow their flight path. Insects, too, are good indicators; large swarms often suggest water is close by. Even in dry landscapes, animal tracks can guide you to waterholes used by wildlife. These tracks often converge towards a common point, which is likely a water source.

Vegetation patterns are another telltale sign of water. Lush, green foliage indicates a higher moisture level in the soil, signaling proximity to water. Trees like willows, cottonwoods, and sycamores generally grow near water bodies like rivers and streams. Ferns and other water-loving plants are also good indicators in forested areas. In deserts, the presence of certain types of cacti or clusters of greenery in an otherwise barren landscape often points to underground water.

Navigating terrain using maps and compasses to locate hidden or remote water bodies is a fundamental survival technique. Topographical maps, in particular, are invaluable. They provide information about the elevation and features of the surroundings, helping identify potential water sources such as valleys, canyons, and riverbeds. Valleys and depressions tend to collect water runoff, making them prime locations to search. Learning how to read these maps accurately and understanding the symbols used for different geographical features can significantly increase your chances of success.

Using a compass in conjunction with a map allows you to navigate even the most challenging terrains. Identify your starting point on the map and plot a route to the nearest likely water source. Keep track of your bearings and distances traveled. This method ensures you don't get lost while searching for water, which is crucial when every drop counts.

In emergency situations, strategies for quickly finding water using improvised tools can be lifesaving. For instance, creating a solar still can help extract water from soil or plant material. Dig a hole in a sunny area, place a container in the center, and cover the hole with plastic sheeting anchored by rocks around the edges. Place a small stone in the center of the plastic sheet to create a dip directly above the container. As the sun heats the soil, water vapor will condense on the underside of the plastic and drip into the container. Another quick method involves using absorbent cloths to collect morning dew. Tie the cloths around your ankles and walk through tall grass or vegetation at dawn. The dew will soak into the cloths, which you can then wring out into a container.

Improvised tools like scooping devices made from bark, large leaves, or even clothing can aid in collecting rainwater or digging for underground water. Carrying multipurpose items like a poncho or tarpaulin can also be beneficial for collecting rainwater. Simply stretch the tarp between trees or poles, allowing it to funnel water into your containers during a downpour.

Recognizing topographical features that suggest the presence of water can further improve your chances of finding hydration. Natural formations such as canyons, gullies, and ravines often contain water, especially after rainfall. During dry seasons, follow these waterways downstream where pools or damp patches may linger. Rock crevices and indentations can hold rainwater long after the surface has dried. In coastal areas, fresh water can sometimes be found inland from the high tide line by digging in the sand behind the first dune.

In mountainous regions, water is more likely to be found at the base of cliffs or rock formations where it collects after running down slopes. Look for dark stains on cliff faces, indicating water seepage. Snow-capped peaks are another obvious source; melting snow provides a steady trickle down the mountainsides. Always approach such sources cautiously as loose rocks and sudden snowmelt can pose hazards.

A thorough understanding of these methods and techniques increases your preparedness for survival scenarios. Identifying key indicators like wildlife behavior, vegetation patterns, and topographical features, combined with effective use of navigation tools and improvised strategies, equips you to find safe and reliable water sources. Remember, knowledge and preparation are your best allies in ensuring access to clean water when conventional supplies are unavailable.

Water purification techniques

Purifying water to make it safe for consumption in survival scenarios is essential knowledge for anyone interested in emergency preparedness. Understanding the different methods and their applications can significantly increase your chances of staying healthy in challenging situations.

One of the most effective and straightforward methods to purify water is boiling. Boiling water kills harmful microorganisms, including bacteria, viruses, and parasites, making it safe to drink. To ensure the water is adequately purified, bring it to a full rolling boil for at least five minutes. Some experts recommend boiling for longer, especially if you're unsure about the water's contamination level. If you're at an elevation above 6,500 feet, extend the boiling time to three minutes due to lower boiling points at higher altitudes (Ellis, 2020).

When boiling water, it's crucial to consider fuel conservation, as you may have limited resources in a survival scenario. Use small, efficient fires or portable stoves designed for minimal fuel consumption. Additionally, cover your pot to reduce heat loss and speed up the boiling process. Despite being highly effective, boiling has a downside: it removes oxygen from the water, resulting in a flat taste. You can improve its flavor by pouring it back and forth between two containers or shaking it in a sealed container to reintroduce oxygen.

Chemical treatments are another viable option for purifying water. Purification tablets, such as iodine or chlorine dioxide, are widely available, compact, and easy to use. To treat water with iodine tablets, add one to two tablets per quart of water, shake the container, and let it sit for at least twenty minutes before drinking. Be aware that iodine-treated water may have a darker color and an unpleasant taste, which can be masked by adding a powdered drink mix after the waiting period (National Park Service, 2017). Chlorine dioxide tablets work similarly, and both types are effective against bacteria and viruses but may take longer to work on certain parasites.

However, chemical treatments come with potential risks. Iodine is not recommended for pregnant women, people with thyroid issues, or those with iodine hypersensitivity (National Park Service, 2017). Long-term use of iodine can also have adverse health effects. Therefore, it's essential to follow the manufacturer's instructions carefully and consult a physician if you have any concerns. Another consideration is the treatment time, which can vary depending on water temperature, pH, and cloudiness. Always allow adequate contact time to ensure the water is safe to drink.

Portable filtration systems offer another method for purifying water. These systems come in various shapes and sizes, often incorporating charcoal or ceramic filters to remove contaminants. Most filters work by drawing water through a hose from the source, passing it through the filter, and then expelling clean water through a separate hose. It's important to avoid cross-contamination by keeping the intake hose separate from the clean output hose (Ellis, 2020). Portable filters are particularly useful when dealing with murky or dirty water, as they effectively remove sediment and tannins.

However, filtration systems have their drawbacks. Filters can become clogged quickly, especially when dealing with dirty water, reducing their effectiveness and requiring frequent maintenance or replacement. When choosing a filter, consider the cost of replacement parts and the overall durability of the system. Some filters can be cleaned, while others need complete replacement once clogged. As with all technical equipment, proper care and adherence to the manufacturer's instructions are crucial for optimal performance.

Combining different purification methods can enhance the efficacy of making water safe for consumption. For instance, you can use a portable filter to remove larger particles and then apply a chemical treatment or boil the filtered water to kill any remaining microorganisms. This multi-step approach ensures that your water is as clean as possible, providing an extra layer of safety.

Storing water safely

Proper water storage is crucial for ensuring long-term survival preparedness. In extreme scenarios such as natural disasters or societal breakdowns, the ability to safely store and preserve water can mean the difference between life and death. This subpoint explores the vital aspects of effective water storage, including selecting appropriate containers, maintaining water quality, identifying suitable storage locations, and securing stored water.

To begin with, choosing durable, safe containers is essential. When selecting containers, consider their material, capacity, and purpose. Food-grade plastic and stainless steel are excellent choices because they do not leach harmful chemicals into the water. Additionally, these materials are robust and resistant to cracks or breaks. Containers should come in various sizes to meet different needs, from small bottles for personal use to large barrels for family supplies. Smaller containers are more manageable for daily usage, while larger ones are ideal for bulk storage. Also, ensure that all containers have airtight lids to prevent contamination.

Maintaining water quality is another critical aspect of water storage. Over time, even properly stored water can degrade if not managed correctly. One effective way to maintain water quality is through rotation. Regularly rotating your stored water ensures that it remains fresh. A good rule of thumb is to replace the water every six months. Marking the filling date on each container can help keep track of when it's time to rotate.

Using additives can also aid in preserving water quality. Unscented household bleach is a common additive; adding two drops per quart of water can help kill bacteria and viruses. However, it's important to follow recommended guidelines to avoid over-chlorinating the water. Additionally, there are commercial water preservatives available that can extend the shelf life of stored water up to five years. Regular inspection of the containers is equally important. Checking for leaks, cracks, or any signs of contamination will ensure that your water supply remains safe and potable.

Selecting the right storage locations is also pivotal. It's crucial to store water in areas protected from temperature extremes and sunlight exposure. Indoor storage locations should be cool, dark places like basements or closets. These areas typically maintain a consistent temperature and are shielded from direct light, both of which prevent the growth of algae and bacteria.

For outdoor storage, it's essential to place containers in shaded areas away from direct sunlight. If possible, burying containers can provide additional insulation against temperature fluctuations. Ensure that outdoor storage sites are elevated or have proper drainage to avoid flooding and contamination during heavy rains.

Lastly, securing your stored water is fundamental in preventing contamination and unauthorized access. Concealing water supplies serves as a deterrent against theft and helps protect your resources in times of crisis. Simple strategies, such as covering containers with tarps or storing them in less obvious locations, can make a significant difference.

Using locks or tamper-proof seals on larger containers adds an extra layer of security. For smaller containers, consider using locked cabinets or storage rooms.

Keeping a detailed inventory of your water storage can help monitor usage and quickly identify any discrepancies.

Wrapping Up

In challenging survival situations, knowing how to source, purify, and store water can be the key to staying alive and healthy. This chapter has equipped you with essential skills to locate natural water sources by recognizing wildlife behavior and vegetation patterns, using topographical maps and compasses, and employing emergency techniques like solar stills and dew collection. You have also learned effective purification methods, such as boiling, chemical treatments, and portable filtration systems, ensuring you can make any found water safe for consumption.

Properly storing water is equally important to maintaining a reliable supply. The chapter covered selecting durable containers, maintaining water quality through rotation and additives, and choosing optimal storage locations protected from temperature extremes and contaminants. Lastly, it emphasized securing your stored water to prevent unauthorized access. With this knowledge, you'll be better prepared to ensure access to clean water under any circumstances, enhancing your overall readiness and survival capabilities.

Reference List

Ellis, C. (2020, March 25). *How to Purify Water» Wilderness Awareness School* . Wilderness Awareness School. https://wildernessawareness.org/articles/how-to-purify-water-water-purification-process/

Krebs, J. (2023, August 21). *A Survival Expert's Best Tricks for Finding Water* . Backpacker. https://www.backpacker.com/survival/survival-skills/how-to-find-water-desert-survival-expert-advice/

National Park Service. (2017). *Two Ways to Purify Water (U.S. National Park Service)* . Nps.gov. https://www.nps.gov/articles/2wayspurifywater.htm

Williams, T. (2023, June 27). *Your survival guide on how to find water in the wilderness* . Desert Island Survival. https://www.desertislandsurvival.com/how-to-find-water/

Chapter Seven

Self-Defense and Security

Self-defense and security are fundamental aspects of personal safety, critical in preparing for potential threats. Being equipped with the right techniques and tools can make a significant difference in protecting yourself and your loved ones. This chapter delves into various methods and strategies to enhance your preparedness and response during dangerous situations, ensuring you can effectively safeguard your well-being and that of others.

Throughout this chapter, you will explore practical self-defense tactics that start with the basics of situational awareness. You'll learn how to recognize and assess potential threats early on, enhancing your ability to avoid danger. The chapter also covers essential physical techniques, such as martial arts moves and targeting vulnerable points on an attacker's body. Moreover, it emphasizes the importance of non-violent de-escalation strategies to prevent conflicts from escalating. Additionally, you'll find valuable advice on fortifying your home against intruders, selecting appropriate self-defense tools, and maintaining them properly. By understanding and implementing these comprehensive measures, you'll build a robust defense framework for various scenarios.

Personal Self-Defense Tactics

Developing the skills to defend oneself and others effectively starts with cultivating strong situational awareness. This fundamental aspect of self-defense involves understanding your surroundings and being able to identify potential threats before they escalate. By training yourself to constantly observe your environment, you become more attuned to subtle changes that may indicate danger. For example, noticing a person lingering around a car park or a sudden shift in crowd behavior at an event can signal that something is amiss.

This heightened state of awareness also includes assessing escape routes in any situation. Knowing where the exits are or identifying potential safe locations provides a critical advantage if a quick getaway becomes necessary. Regularly scanning the environment for these details helps embed this habit into your daily routine, making it second nature over time.

Another crucial component of situational awareness is recognizing suspicious behaviors. People who exhibit unusual body language, like excessive nervousness or scanning their surroundings intensely, might be up to no good. Trusting your instincts when something feels off can sometimes be the difference between avoiding a confrontation and becoming a victim. Schools, parks, and public transport are typical places where maintaining situational awareness can significantly improve personal security.

Moving beyond awareness, learning basic martial arts moves and self-defense tactics provides practical tools for physical confrontations. Strikes and blocks form the foundation of most self-defense techniques. Practicing these moves repeatedly helps develop muscle memory, allowing you to react swiftly and efficiently during an actual threat. Simple maneuvers like a well-executed punch or kick can create the critical seconds needed to escape from an attacker.

Understanding the body's vulnerable points, such as the eyes, nose, throat, and groin, further enhances these techniques. Targeting these areas can incapacitate an assailant long enough for you to get away. For instance, a forceful strike to the nose can stun an attacker, providing you the opportunity to flee.

In addition to physical techniques, mastering de-escalation strategies is just as important. Not all conflicts need to end in violence. Learning how to communicate assertively and calmly under pressure can often diffuse a potentially dangerous situation. Techniques such as maintaining a non-threatening stance, using verbal judo to deflect aggression, and demonstrating confidence without aggression can prevent a confrontation from escalating. Effective communication skills are powerful tools in any self-defense arsenal, as they can help avoid physical altercations altogether.

Regular training in these self-defense techniques not only improves proficiency but also builds confidence. Regular practice sessions provide a controlled environment to refine your skills, making them more reliable under stress. Whether through a local dojo, self-defense workshops, or even online tutorials, consistent practice ensures that your responses become automatic. The psychological benefit of knowing you have the skills to protect yourself cannot be overstated; it fosters a sense of empowerment and readiness.

Beyond individual preparedness, consider engaging in community training programs or group classes. These settings offer the advantage of learning from others' experiences, which can provide valuable insights and enhance your own techniques. Additionally, practicing with different partners simulates a variety of real-world scenarios, further improving your adaptability and response times.

It's also invaluable to understand that self-defense is a holistic practice. Physical readiness must be complemented by mental and emotional preparedness. Martial arts training, for instance, teaches practitioners to maintain mental presence and calmness in the face of adversity, reducing the likelihood of panic during a threatening situation. This mental conditioning translates into everyday life, promoting a mindset that remains vigilant yet composed.

Safe Home Fortification Practices

Enhancing home security measures to protect against intruders and threats is vital for ensuring the safety of your household. This subpoint will cover various strategies you can adopt to bolster your home's defenses, focusing on securing entry points, creating safe rooms, and installing surveillance cameras.

Securing Entry Points

The first step in fortifying your home is to secure all entry points. Doors and windows are often the primary targets for intruders. Begin with reinforcing doors by installing sturdy deadbolts and security bars. Deadbolts add an additional layer of protection beyond standard locks, making it more challenging for intruders to break in. Security bars can be installed on both doors and windows, especially those that are less visible and might be targeted.

For windows, consider utilizing window security film or shatter-resistant glass. These materials help prevent easy breakage, deterring would-be intruders. Moreover, using key-operated levers for windows adds an extra barrier, reducing the likelihood of forced entry.

Motion sensor lights are another effective deterrent. When strategically placed around your home's exterior, these lights illuminate whenever movement is detected, startling potential intruders. They also serve as a warning signal, alerting you and your neighbors to possible threats. Additionally, planting thorny bushes near ground-level windows can act as natural barriers, discouraging attempts to access your home through these vulnerable points.

Creating Safe Rooms

Designating a safe room within your home provides a refuge during emergencies. A safe room should be located in an easily accessible area but hidden from plain view. Reinforce this space with solid walls and a sturdy door to ensure it can withstand forced entry.

Stock your safe room with essential supplies such as water, non-perishable food, medical kits, and tools. Communication devices like a phone or two-way radio are crucial for contacting authorities. Establish clear communication protocols among household members so everyone knows how to react and where to go during an intrusion. Regularly rehearse these protocols to ensure everyone is familiar with the steps to take in case of an emergency.

Installing Surveillance Cameras

Surveillance cameras play a significant role in monitoring and protecting vulnerable areas of your home. Install cameras at key locations such as front and back doors, driveways, and any other points of entry. Opt for cameras with night vision capabilities to ensure round-the-clock surveillance.

Modern surveillance systems offer features like motion detection and real-time alerts sent directly to your smartphone. This allows you to monitor your property remotely, providing peace of mind even when you're not at home. Visible cameras also act as a deterrent, making would-be intruders think twice before targeting your home.

Choosing and Maintaining Weapons

When it comes to self-defense, choosing the right tools and ensuring they are properly maintained is crucial. This section will provide guidance on selecting suitable self-defense tools and caring for them effectively.

Understanding the types of defensive weapons available is the first step. Firearms are a popular choice due to their ability to neutralize threats from a distance. However, owning and using a firearm requires a thorough understanding of safety protocols and responsible gun ownership. Melee weapons like knives or batons can also be effective, particularly in close-quarters situations. Non-lethal options, such as pepper spray and tasers, offer a means to incapacitate an assailant without causing permanent harm. For instance, Taser devices are widely used by law enforcement and are designed to provide personal protection while minimizing long-term injury (*TASER Self-Defense*, n.d.).

Once you've selected your weapon, proper storage is essential. Firearms should be stored unloaded and locked in a secure place, accessible only to authorized users. Melee weapons and non-lethal tools should also be kept in places that prevent accidental access, especially by children. Regular maintenance ensures that these tools are functional when needed. Cleaning firearms periodically prevents malfunctions due to dirt buildup, while checking the condition of melee weapons and pepper spray canisters helps avoid failure during critical moments.

Training is indispensable for anyone who owns a self-defense tool. Accuracy and proficiency with a firearm, for example, depend heavily on regular practice. Visiting shooting ranges and participating in drills can enhance one's skill level. Similarly, practicing with melee weapons or tasers ensures the user can deploy them quickly and effectively under stress. Professional instruction provides valuable insights into advanced techniques and safe handling practices, fostering a higher level of competency.

Incorporating weapon training into overall self-defense strategies is vital. Knowing how to use a weapon is only part of the equation; integrating this knowledge into broader defensive tactics maximizes preparedness. This includes understanding situational awareness, recognizing potential threats early, and knowing when and how to use your chosen tool effectively. Regularly updating your training regimen and staying informed about new self-defense technologies and methods will keep your skills sharp and relevant.

Final Thoughts

Throughout this chapter, we have explored various techniques and tools crucial for protecting yourself and your loved ones. From developing strong situational awareness to learning basic self-defense tactics, these skills help you recognize potential threats and respond effectively. Understanding the importance of escape routes and recognizing suspicious behavior can give you a significant advantage in avoiding danger. Moreover, mastering physical defense moves and targeting vulnerable points on an assailant's body can provide the critical seconds needed to ensure your safety.

We also delved into home fortification practices, emphasizing the need to secure entry points, create safe rooms, and install surveillance cameras. These measures are vital for enhancing the security of your household. Choosing the right self-defense tools and maintaining them properly ensures they are ready when needed. Regular training in both physical and weapon-based self-defense builds confidence and readiness, helping you remain composed and act swiftly during emergencies. By integrating these strategies into your daily life, you can significantly enhance your preparedness and ability to protect yourself and your loved ones.

Reference List

Developing Awareness and Self-Defense Skills through Martial Arts . (n.d.). Martialartswa.com. https://martialartswa.com/blog/developing-awareness-and-selfdefense-skills-through-martial-arts-096

Edwards, R. (2020, October 15). *10 Simple Ways to Secure Your New Home* . SafeWise. https://www.safewise.com/blog/10-simple-ways-to-secure-your-new-home/

How can guns be countered by melee combat without raw-ability or exceptional explanations? (n.d.). Worldbuilding Stack Exchange. Retrieved July 29, 2024, from https://worldbuilding.stackexchange.com/questions/139429/how-can-guns-be-countered-by-melee-combat-without-raw-ability-or-exceptional-exp

Martial Arts and Self-Defense: Why Every Child Should Learn | Infinity Taekwondo . (n.d.). Infinity-Tkd.com. Retrieved July 29, 2024, from https://infinity-tkd.com/2024/05/31/martial-arts-and-self-defense-why-every-child-should-learn/

TASER Self-Defense . (n.d.). TASER Self-Defense. https://taser.com/

medallions. (2024, April 24). *Why Inadequate Home Security Puts You at Risk* . Medallion   Security.   https://www.medallionsecurity.com/why-inadequate-home-security-puts-you-at-risk/

Chapter Eight

Medical Preparedness and First Aid

Handling medical emergencies efficiently requires both knowledge and preparation, which are key elements of medical preparedness and first aid. This chapter delves into the essential components of setting up a basic medical kit, outlining the necessary tools and supplies that can make a critical difference in survival situations. It emphasizes the importance of having a well-rounded medical kit and maintaining it to ensure effectiveness during emergencies. By addressing the practical aspects of building and organizing a medical kit, readers will be better equipped to manage health-related issues when access to professional medical care is limited or unavailable.

The chapter provides detailed guidance on selecting essential items for a basic medical kit, from bandages and antiseptic solutions to medications and tools like tweezers and scissors. It underscores the necessity of each item and its role in treating minor injuries, preventing infections, and managing common health problems. Additionally, the chapter offers insights into organizing and routinely maintaining the medical kit to keep it functional and ready for use. Through this comprehensive approach, readers will gain valuable skills and confidence in handling a wide array of medical emergencies, enhancing their overall preparedness for extreme scenarios.

Setting up a Basic Medical Kit

Equipping readers with the necessary tools and supplies for medical emergencies is a foundational aspect of any survival strategy. Understanding what to include in a basic medical kit and ensuring it is well-maintained can significantly enhance one's ability to handle various medical emergencies effectively.

Essential Items for a Basic Medical Kit

A comprehensive medical kit is crucial for addressing health-related issues during emergency situations. Whether you are preparing for natural disasters, societal breakdowns, or other extreme scenarios, having a well-rounded medical kit can make all the difference. Essential items for a basic medical kit should cover a wide range of potential medical problems.

First, consider including bandages of various sizes and types, such as adhesive bandages, nonstick sterile bandages, and elastic wrap bandages. These items are crucial for treating cuts, abrasions, and other minor injuries. Adhesive tape, which helps secure bandages, and butterfly bandages for more serious cuts are also important additions.

Antiseptic solutions and antibiotic ointments are critical for cleaning wounds and preventing infections. Including antiseptic wipes can provide a quick and effective way to clean hands or equipment before handling injuries. Medications, another key component, should consist of pain relievers like acetaminophen or ibuprofen and antihistamines for allergic reactions. Anti-diarrhea medication and laxatives can help address gastrointestinal issues, while hydrocortisone cream can be used for insect bites or rashes.

Tools such as tweezers, scissors, and a thermometer are indispensable for performing basic medical procedures. A breathing barrier or surgical mask can be essential for providing rescue breaths during CPR without direct mouth-to-mouth contact. An instant cold pack and emergency blanket can be useful for dealing with sprains, strains, and hypothermia respectively. Gloves, preferably non-latex, should always be worn when treating open wounds to prevent contamination.

Understanding the Importance of Having a Well-Rounded Medical Kit

In emergency situations, access to professional medical care may be limited or entirely unavailable. Therefore, having a well-rounded medical kit allows individuals to manage minor injuries and illnesses on their own. This could mean the difference between a manageable situation and a life-threatening one.

A medical kit prepares you not just for injuries, but for a variety of health issues that could arise. It ensures you have immediate access to necessary supplies, which can help stabilize a condition until professional help is available. Knowing that you have a robust medical kit at your disposal provides peace of mind and promotes a proactive approach to health and safety.

Identifying Essential Items

Having a list of essential items is crucial for assembling an effective medical kit. Here are some must-haves:

1. **Bandages and Dressings:** Include absorbent compress dressings, assorted adhesive bandages, gauze rolls, and sterile gauze pads. These help manage different wounds, from minor scratches to more significant lacerations.

2. **Antiseptics and Antibiotics:** Stock small packets of antibiotic ointments and antiseptic wipes. These aid in cleaning wounds and preventing infection.

3. **Medications:** Pain relievers, anti-inflammatory drugs, antihistamines, and basic medications for digestive issues are vital. Don't forget personal medication and aspirin, considering its life-saving potential during chest pain (Mayo Clinic Staff, 2018).

4. **Tools:** Scissors, tweezers, a digital thermometer, and a needle for splinters. Tools aid in managing wounds and removing foreign objects.

5. **Protective Gear:** Non-latex gloves and a breathing barrier are essential for keeping both the caregiver and patient safe.

6. **Miscellaneous:** Emergency blankets, cold packs, eye wash solution, and burn cream are also advisable additions.

Organizing and Maintaining the Medical Kit

After gathering the necessary supplies, it's essential to organize the contents methodically to ensure quick and easy access during emergencies. Use compartments or labeled bags to categorize items, separating bandages, medications, tools, and protective gear. Keeping a first-aid manual within the kit can be very helpful, offering step-by-step guidance during crises (American Red Cross, 2023).

Maintenance of the medical kit is equally important. Regularly check the contents to ensure nothing is expired or used up. Some items like medications and antiseptic solutions can lose their efficacy over time. Replace these as needed, and make sure batteries in devices like digital thermometers still work.

Implementing a routine check-up and restocking schedule is beneficial. Mark the date when you last checked or used the kit, and plan monthly inspections. This proactive approach guarantees the kit remains functional and ready for use whenever required.

Performing First Aid and CPR

When facing emergencies, knowing essential life-saving techniques can mean the difference between life and death. Basic first aid procedures are imperative to ensure immediate and proper care in the event of common injuries or medical crises. Understanding how to address these situations effectively can mitigate complications and stabilize individuals until professional help arrives. This chapter elucidates such crucial techniques for preppers and survivalists to handle various injuries and emergencies.

Basic First Aid Procedures provide the foundation for addressing common injuries like cuts, burns, fractures, and more. A minor cut, if not treated properly, can lead to unnecessary complications. Start by washing your hands thoroughly before touching the wound to avoid infections. Clean the cut with clear water and mild soap, removing any debris gently. Applying an antiseptic ointment then covering the area with a sterile bandage protects against infection and promotes healing. It's simple yet effective steps like these that form the bedrock of first aid.

Burns require immediate attention to prevent further skin damage. For minor burns, holding the affected area under cool running water for several minutes alleviates pain and minimizes tissue damage. Avoid using ice as it can exacerbate the burn. After cooling, cover the burn with a non-stick, sterile bandage. Over-the-counter pain relievers can help manage discomfort. For severe burns where the skin is charred or blistered extensively, seek emergency medical attention promptly, as these could be life-threatening.

Fractures or broken bones necessitate immobilization to prevent further injury. If you suspect a bone fracture, avoid moving the injured limb. You can create a makeshift splint using sturdy materials like sticks or rolled newspapers, securing it with cloth strips without cutting off circulation. It helps keep the bone aligned until professional medical care is available.

Providing step-by-step instructions on administering first aid correctly ensures readers can act confidently during an emergency. When someone is choking, swift and correct intervention can save a life. The Heimlich maneuver is a well-known technique. Stand behind the person, wrapping your arms around their waist. Make a fist with one hand and place it just above the navel, grasping it with your other hand. Push hard into the abdomen with quick, upward thrusts. Repeat until the object is expelled.

For bleeding wounds, stop the bleeding by applying direct pressure using a clean cloth or bandage. Maintaining steady pressure helps slow blood flow, allowing a clot to form. Elevating the injured area above heart level further reduces bleeding. Keep the person calm and still to prevent exacerbation of the injury. If bleeding continues despite these measures, it's vital to seek emergency medical assistance immediately.

CPR (Cardio-Pulmonary Resuscitation) is a critical skill in life-threatening situations. This technique involves chest compressions and rescue breaths to maintain circulatory flow and oxygenation during cardiac arrest. Performing CPR correctly can significantly enhance the chances of survival. According to the American Red Cross, the initial steps include checking the scene for safety and ensuring personal protective equipment (PPE) is used (American Red Cross, 2019). Once it's safe, check if the person is responsive by shouting and tapping. If unresponsive, call emergency services immediately.

Place the person on their back on a firm surface and begin chest compressions. Position your hands in the center of the chest, keeping your elbows locked. Compress the chest at least 2 inches deep at a rate of 100 to 120 compressions per minute. Allow the chest to return to its normal position after each compression. The American Heart Association emphasizes the need to ensure correct depth and pace to maximize effectiveness (Barrell, 2023).

After 30 compressions, give two rescue breaths. Tilt the person's head back slightly by lifting the chin to open the airway. Pinch the nose shut and make a complete seal over their mouth with yours, delivering a breath lasting about one second each, making sure the chest rises visibly with each breath. Continue this cycle of 30 compressions and two breaths until emergency personnel arrive or an automated external defibrillator (AED) is available.

It's essential to note that CPR techniques vary for infants and children. Use only two fingers for chest compressions on infants, pressing about 1.5 inches deep. For children, use one or both hands depending on their size, compressing about 2 inches. Ensure a gentle approach to avoid causing injury but maintain rhythm and depth to be effective.

Regular training refreshers can help retain proficiency in these skills. Community centers and local health organizations often provide CPR and first aid courses. Practicing these techniques in realistic scenarios can build confidence and readiness to act swiftly and correctly in real emergencies.

Managing Trauma and Infections

In emergency scenarios, having the skills to manage traumatic injuries and infections is crucial for survival. This subpoint aims to equip readers with the knowledge needed to handle such situations effectively. Understanding how to assess and treat traumatic injuries promptly can make the difference between life and death. Similarly, insights into proper wound care and infection prevention are vital in ensuring long-term survival in challenging environments.

Assessing and Treating Traumatic Injuries

In the immediate aftermath of a traumatic injury, swift assessment and treatment are essential. The first step is identifying the nature and severity of the injury. Look for visible signs like open wounds, swelling, or deformity, and assess the patient's level of consciousness and breathing. It's important to determine whether the injury involves bleeding, broken bones, or internal damage. For example, if a person is injured in a car accident, they might have multiple trauma points, including head injuries, fractures, or deep lacerations.

Once the injury is identified, the next step is to provide initial treatment. Controlling bleeding is a priority; use direct pressure and, if necessary, a tourniquet. Immobilize any suspected fractures with splints to prevent further injury. For head injuries, keep the patient still and monitor their condition closely. Swiftly addressing these injuries can stabilize the patient and buy critical time before professional medical help arrives (James & Pennardt, 2023).

Emergency Wound Care

Proper wound care is paramount in preventing infections and complications in survival scenarios. Start by cleaning the wound thoroughly with clean water or a saline solution to remove debris and contaminants. If available, antiseptic solutions can further reduce the risk of infection. After cleaning, apply an appropriate dressing; sterile gauze or clean cloth will suffice if commercial dressings are not available. Secure the dressing with bandages but avoid wrapping too tightly as it could cut off circulation.

In cases where the wound is deep or large, suturing may be necessary. However, this should only be attempted if you have sterile equipment and the know-how to perform the procedure correctly. Otherwise, keep the wound clean and change the dressings regularly. Monitoring the wound for signs of infection like redness, swelling, or pus is crucial. Early detection of infection allows for prompt intervention, including cleaning the wound again, using antibiotic ointments, or in severe cases, administering antibiotics (Andersen, 2019).

Preventative Measures

Preventing infections and diseases in challenging environments requires a proactive approach. Basic hygiene practices like regular handwashing with soap and water play a significant role in reducing the spread of pathogens. In the absence of water, hand sanitizers with at least 60% alcohol can be effective. It's also important to keep living areas clean and free from waste, as unsanitary conditions can harbor bacteria and viruses.

Another key preventative measure is ensuring safe food and water consumption. Boiling water kills most pathogens and makes it safe to drink. Similarly, cooking food thoroughly minimizes the risk of foodborne illnesses. Avoid consuming raw or undercooked foods, particularly in environments where healthcare access is limited. Vaccinations, when available, are another layer of defense against infectious diseases. Keeping up-to-date with vaccinations reduces the risk of contracting and spreading diseases like tetanus, hepatitis, and influenza.

Identifying Common Diseases

Recognizing common diseases in survival scenarios enables timely and appropriate responses. Some prevalent diseases include gastrointestinal infections, respiratory illnesses, and vector-borne diseases like malaria. Gastrointestinal infections often result from contaminated food or water and present symptoms like diarrhea, vomiting, and abdominal pain. Rapid dehydration from such infections can be fatal if not treated promptly. Rehydration solutions, either commercially prepared or homemade with clean water, salt, and sugar, can combat dehydration.

Respiratory illnesses, ranging from the common cold to pneumonia, can escalate quickly without proper care. Symptoms like persistent cough, fever, and difficulty breathing warrant immediate attention. Providing a warm environment, ensuring adequate rest, and keeping the patient hydrated are basic care steps. In cases of severe respiratory distress, medical attention is crucial.

Vector-borne diseases, spread by insects like mosquitoes and ticks, are another concern. Protecting yourself with insect repellent, wearing long sleeves and pants, and using mosquito nets can reduce the risk of exposure. Recognizing symptoms early, such as high fever, chills, and joint pain in the case of malaria, allows for timely treatment with antimalarial medications.

Demonstrating Wound Cleaning, Dressing, and Infection Control Methods

Effective wound management in emergencies often requires demonstrating proper techniques. Begin with cleaning the wound using clean water or saline. Gently flush out dirt and debris, taking care not to scrub aggressively, which can cause more damage. Use sterilized instruments if available, or ensure any improvised tools are as clean as possible. Once cleaned, pat the wound dry with a sterile cloth or gauze.

Next, apply an appropriate dressing. Sterile gauze pads offer good coverage, but if unavailable, a clean piece of cloth can work. Fold the cloth to fit the wound size and place it directly over the cleaned area. Secure with adhesive tape or bandages, ensuring the dressing stays in place without restricting blood flow.

Infection control methods include changing the dressing regularly, ideally once daily or whenever it becomes wet or dirty. Encourage the patient to avoid touching or scratching the wound, as this can introduce new bacteria. Wash hands thoroughly before and after handling the wound to maintain hygiene. Keeping an eye on the wound for signs of infection and addressing any changes swiftly is critical in preventing complications.

Developing Long-term Care Plans

For extended survival scenarios, creating comprehensive medical care plans is essential. Start by assessing ongoing healthcare needs, considering chronic conditions that require regular medication or monitoring. Stockpiling essential medications and supplies ensures continuity of care during prolonged emergencies. Planning should also encompass potential medical emergencies. Identify nearby resources like clinics or hospitals and understand their accessibility in different crisis scenarios. Establishing a network with other survivors can provide support and share medical knowledge.

Regular training and practice in first aid and emergency medical procedures enhance readiness. Conducting mock drills and reviewing medical supplies periodically keeps everyone prepared for real emergencies. Having detailed care plans documented and easily accessible ensures that everyone involved knows their roles and responsibilities in maintaining health and managing medical issues long-term.

Wrapping Up

In this chapter, we delved into the essential knowledge and skills required to handle medical emergencies effectively. We discussed the importance of setting up a basic medical kit, ensuring it is well-stocked with necessary supplies like bandages, antiseptics, and medications. With a robust medical kit at hand, you can address minor injuries and health issues promptly, providing immediate care until professional help arrives. We also covered critical first aid techniques, including how to treat cuts, burns, fractures, and choking incidents, emphasizing the need for proper training and routine practice.

Knowing how to manage trauma and prevent infections is vital for survival in extreme scenarios. From controlling bleeding and immobilizing fractures to cleaning wounds and preventing contamination, these skills can make a significant difference in emergency situations. Regular maintenance and thorough understanding of your medical kit's contents will ensure you are always prepared to act swiftly. By mastering these fundamentals, you're not just enhancing your preparedness but also fostering confidence and resilience in facing any medical crisis that arises.

Reference List

American Red Cross. (2023). *Make a First Aid Kit* . American Red Cross. https://www.redcross.org/get-help/how-to-prepare-for-emergencies/anatomy-of-a-first-aid-kit.html

American Red Cross. (2019). *CPR Steps* . Red Cross; American Red Cross. https://www.redcross.org/take-a-class/cpr/performing-cpr/cpr-steps

Andersen, B. M. (2019). *Prevention of Postoperative Wound Infections* . Prevention and Control of Infections in Hospitals. https://doi.org/10.1007/978-3-319-99921-0_33

Barrell, A. (2023, May 22). *How to perform CPR: Guidelines, procedure, and ratio* . Medical News Today. https://www.medicalnewstoday.com/articles/324712

James, D., & Pennardt, A. M. (2023, May 31). *Trauma Care Principles* . PubMed; StatPearls Publishing. https://www.ncbi.nlm.nih.gov/books/NBK547757/

Mayo Clinic Staff. (2018). *First-aid kits: Stock supplies that can save lives* . Mayo Clinic. https://www.mayoclinic.org/first-aid/first-aid-kits/basics/art-20056673

Chapter Nine

Shelter and Safe Havens

Creating and maintaining safe living spaces during crises is essential for survival. Whether facing natural disasters, economic collapse, or societal breakdowns, having a secure and reliable shelter can significantly impact your well-being and chances of enduring challenging times. The process involves not only constructing temporary shelters using available resources but also choosing optimal locations that provide natural protection against harsh weather conditions and potential threats. The key to establishing these refuges lies in the strategic selection of materials and placement, ensuring that they offer maximum security and comfort. From simple lean-to shelters built with wood and tarps to more complex structures reinforced with logs and debris, each type serves a specific purpose depending on the environment and immediate needs.

In this chapter, we delve into various methods of creating effective shelters that keep you safe from environmental hazards and potential intruders. We will explore the best practices for selecting suitable locations, including avoiding flood-prone areas and positioning shelters to benefit from natural windbreaks and sunlight. Additionally, we'll discuss the efficient use of available materials to enhance the durability and stability of your shelter, as well as techniques for securing it against wind, rain, and other environmental factors. You will learn about the importance of reinforcing structural components, setting up makeshift doors, and implementing drainage systems to prevent flooding. This chapter aims to equip you with practical knowledge and strategies to ensure that your shelter remains a safe haven throughout any crisis.

Building Temporary Shelters

In times of crisis, providing immediate protection and offering temporary living solutions is paramount. The first step toward achieving this is selecting areas with natural cover and minimal exposure to the elements for optimal shelter placement. Natural features such as rock formations, dense tree canopies, and elevated grounds offer several advantages. They provide a windbreak, minimize rainfall impact, and reduce visibility to potential threats. These natural covers act as the first line of defense against harsh weather conditions, allowing for relatively safer and more comfortable shelter locations.

Choosing the right location is crucial. Low-lying areas might seem ideal due to their flat land but can be prone to flooding. Instead, aim for slightly raised terrain to avoid water accumulation around your shelter. Also, consider the sun's path. Position your shelter where it receives morning sunlight to dry out any moisture from the night and offers shade during the peak heat of the day.

Next, using available resources efficiently can greatly enhance your shelter's durability and security. Wood, tarp, and debris are common materials you might find in your immediate environment. They are versatile and can be used to construct various types of temporary shelters. For instance, large branches and logs can serve as the main framework, while smaller twigs and leaves can be woven together to create walls that insulate the shelter. Tarp, if available, is excellent for creating waterproof coverings.

To build a sturdy shelter quickly, start by constructing a basic frame with the strongest wooden pieces you can find. Lean-to shelters are easily constructed and require only a few materials: two sturdy poles or trees, a long cross pole, and additional branches or tarp for covering. Secure the structure with vines or rope to ensure stability. Make sure the walls are at an angle that allows rainwater to run off rather than pool on top, which could compromise the shelter's integrity.

Securing the shelter against wind, rain, and other environmental factors is essential to ensure its stability. Consider the direction of prevailing winds and build your shelter with its back facing the wind. This will prevent the wind from directly entering the shelter and reduce its impact on the structure. Additionally, reinforcing the roof with extra layers of leaves, tarps, or even earth can provide added protection against rainfall.

An important guideline here is to dig a small trench around the perimeter of your shelter. This helps divert rainwater away, preventing flooding inside. It also acts as a simple drainage system, reducing the risk of standing water around your living area, which could attract insects and pests.

Implementing safety protocols enhances the shelter's ability to protect its occupants. Reinforcing the structure is critical, especially in environments prone to severe weather. Use thicker branches for support beams and lash them together tightly. If possible, use nails or screws for more permanent reinforcement. Adding barriers of rocks or heavy logs around the base can prevent the structure from shifting or collapsing during strong winds.

Conduct periodic checks to ensure all bindings are secure and nothing has loosened over time. A well-reinforced shelter not only stands better against environmental threats but also provides peace of mind, allowing inhabitants to focus on other survival tasks.

For added protection, create a makeshift doorway using a large branch or board that can be moved into place when needed. This keeps unwanted animals out and maintains the shelter's internal temperature by limiting airflow in colder climates. Furthermore, setting up a small fire pit outside of the shelter can serve dual purposes: providing warmth and acting as a deterrent against wildlife.

Maintaining a clean and organized shelter environment is also part of the overall safety protocol. Ensure that tools and supplies are neatly stored and easily accessible. This prevents accidents like tripping over equipment and ensures that everything is at hand in case of an emergency. Regularly clean the area to avoid attracting pests, and keep food stores securely packed.

Finally, always have an exit plan. Knowing how to quickly dismantle your shelter and relocate if necessary can be pivotal in certain situations. Whether it's due to changing weather conditions or discovering a safer location nearby, being prepared to move promptly can make all the difference.

Retrofitting Homes for Disasters

Transforming existing homes into disaster-resistant and secure living spaces is a crucial step towards ensuring safety during crises. A first and essential task in this transformation process is conducting a thorough home assessment, which helps to identify weak areas and potential threats. This involves evaluating the structure of your home, checking for vulnerabilities such as cracks in walls, unstable foundations, outdated electrical systems, and other points of concern that could compromise the integrity of your shelter during a disaster. Consider hiring a professional inspector if possible, as they can provide an expert eye to spot issues you might overlook.

Once the assessment is complete and vulnerabilities are identified, the next step is to install safeguards to enhance your home's resilience. Start with securing windows, doors, and roofs, as these are common entry points for damage during high winds, storms, or break-ins. For instance, reinforcing doors with solid deadbolts and sturdy frames can significantly improve security. Windows should be fitted with storm shutters or impact-resistant glass to withstand strong winds and flying debris. The roof, being the most exposed part of the house, requires special attention; ensure it is well-maintained, and consider adding hurricane straps or clips to keep it firmly attached to the main structure.

Creating designated safe areas within the home is another vital aspect of preparing for emergencies. These safe zones should be strategically located in structurally sound parts of the house—often basements or interior rooms without windows. Stock these areas with essential supplies such as non-perishable food, water, medical kits, flashlights, batteries, and other emergency necessities. It's also wise to include some form of entertainment or comfort items to help reduce stress during prolonged stays in these zones. Remember, preparing these areas before a crisis occurs can save valuable time and potentially lives.

Establishing reliable communication methods is equally important to ensure you remain connected during disasters. Traditional landlines might fail, so having multiple forms of communication is advisable. Invest in battery-powered radios to stay informed about weather updates and emergency instructions. Mobile phones should be fully charged, and portable chargers or power banks should be readily available. Family members should agree on a specific meeting point outside the home and have a list of emergency contacts saved both digitally and on paper. Two-way radios can be beneficial for family communication, especially if cellular networks become unreliable.

Beyond these primary steps, integrating community resources and support networks can further enhance your home's preparedness. Engage with local emergency services to understand available resources and support systems. Participate in community drills and training sessions to stay updated on best practices. Additionally, forming alliances with neighbors can create a supportive network where everyone looks out for each other's safety and wellbeing.

To sum up, transforming your home into a disaster-resistant haven requires a multifaceted approach. Conducting a comprehensive home assessment sets the foundation by identifying and addressing weaknesses. Installing robust safeguards such as reinforced doors, storm shutters, and secure roofs fortifies the structure. Designated safe zones stocked with essentials provide immediate refuge during emergencies. Establishing diverse communication methods ensures you remain connected and informed. By incorporating these strategies and leveraging community support, you can create a safer living space that stands resilient against crises.

Camouflaging and Securing Shelters

When preparing shelters to be concealed from potential threats, it's crucial to incorporate natural materials and colors that blend seamlessly with the surrounding environment. Imagine a shelter in a densely wooded area; utilizing bark, leaves, and naturally occurring hues like greens, browns, and grays can help make the shelter inconspicuous. Consider covering the exterior with mud or clay found nearby, as this not only camouflages the structure but also provides additional insulation. This method follows principles seen in wildlife habitats where creatures use available resources for concealment. For instance, birds construct nests using twigs and leaves to blend into trees. Similarly, your shelter should mimic the colors and textures of its surroundings to avoid detection.

Securing entry points is another essential aspect of maintaining a safe haven. Doors and windows are common vulnerabilities in any shelter. Installing durable locks is one of the first steps in fortifying these entry points. Choose high-quality padlocks and deadbolts designed to withstand significant force. In addition to physical barriers, implementing alarms can provide an added layer of security. Basic DIY alarm systems, such as those utilizing tripwires and bells, can be effective and cost-efficient. Alternatively, more advanced electronic alarms can alert you to unauthorized access through sound or notifications on mobile devices. Surveillance methods, including cameras or strategic peepholes, enable constant monitoring of entry points. Even simple measures like using reflective surfaces positioned to give a view of blind spots can increase awareness of one's surroundings.

Setting up warning systems and barriers around the shelter further enhances protection. Physical barriers like fences or thorny bushes can act as deterrents to would-be intruders. Constructing a perimeter fence using materials like wood or metal is practical. For those preferring a more natural approach, planting thick bushes or hedges creates a natural barrier that is both functional and aesthetically pleasing. Warning systems can range from rudimentary to advanced. Stringing up noise-making objects such as cans or installing motion sensor lights at key points around the shelter can serve as early warnings of approaching danger. These measures create layers of defense that increase reaction time and reduce the likelihood of being taken by surprise.

Implementing defensive strategies is paramount for repelling intruders and ensuring occupant safety. Defensive preparations might include creating escape routes, stockpiling defensive tools, and learning self-defense techniques. Establish multiple escape routes in case the primary exit is compromised. An underground tunnel leading to a secondary location or a disguised backdoor can be lifesaving during an intrusion. Stock defensive tools such as pepper spray, stun guns, or even household items that could be used in defense, like bats or heavy flashlights, within easy reach throughout the shelter. Additionally, consider training in basic self-defense; understanding how to defend oneself physically can empower occupants and provide peace of mind. Strategies might also involve setting up decoys or traps around the property to confuse or hinder intruders, buying precious time for occupants to react or escape.

Final Thoughts

This chapter has provided detailed instructions on creating and maintaining temporary shelters during crises. By selecting areas with natural cover, efficiently using available resources, and reinforcing the structure against harsh weather, we can ensure a secure living space. The placement of shelters, considerations for sun exposure, and essential techniques like building drainage systems all contribute to enhancing the safety and durability of these temporary homes.

We also explored methods for retrofitting existing homes to withstand disasters. Through comprehensive home assessments, installing safeguards, and setting up designated safe zones, you can transform your home into a disaster-resistant haven. Additionally, implementing effective communication strategies and leveraging community resources are vital steps in ensuring overall safety. By mastering these techniques, you can create strong, safe living spaces capable of enduring various crises.

Chapter Ten

Navigating a Post-Apocalyptic World

Surviving in a post-apocalyptic world demands more than just basic survival skills; it requires an adept understanding of new societal norms and the ability to adapt to drastically altered environments. As traditional societal structures break down, new hierarchies, cultural practices, and conflict dynamics emerge, creating a complex and often unpredictable social landscape. To thrive in this environment, one must be keenly observant and ready to navigate these new realities with both strategic alliances and adaptable behaviors. Recognizing the power dynamics at play, respecting diverse cultures, and resolving conflicts peacefully are all crucial elements that can significantly influence one's chances of survival.

This chapter delves into the skills and strategies essential for thriving in a post-apocalyptic world. It examines how to identify and navigate new social hierarchies, offering insights into aligning oneself strategically within these emerging networks. Furthermore, it discusses the importance of cultural adaptation and learning from the traditions and practices of others to foster mutual understanding and community cohesion. Conflict resolution techniques are also explored, highlighting the need for effective communication and mediation to maintain stability. Finally, the chapter emphasizes the development of strong leadership skills, focusing on resilience, ethical behavior, and collaborative decision-making to guide communities toward positive outcomes.

Adapting to New Societal Norms

In a post-apocalyptic world, traditional societal structures and norms will undoubtedly undergo drastic changes. Understanding these shifts is crucial for survival and adaptation. This subpoint delves into recognizing and navigating new social hierarchies, embracing cultural adaptations, resolving conflicts peacefully, and developing leadership skills to thrive in such an environment.

Observing Social Hierarchies

The collapse of civilization often leads to the emergence of new social orders. These new hierarchies may not resemble pre-apocalyptic structures; they can be fluid and based on different criteria. To navigate these new power dynamics effectively, it is vital to keenly observe and analyze social interactions within your community. For instance, who are the decision-makers? Who holds valuable resources or knowledge? Recognizing these key individuals and understanding their influence can help you align yourself strategically and ensure your inclusion within these new social networks.

Power dynamics in post-apocalyptic societies can be based on survival skills, resource control, or even sheer physical strength. It's essential to stay observant and adapt quickly. Form alliances with influential people to secure protection and resources. By understanding and adapting to these new social hierarchies, you can better navigate interpersonal relations, enhance your safety, and increase your chances of survival.

Cultural Adaptation

In the wake of societal collapse, diverse groups of survivors will come together, each bringing their unique cultural practices and beliefs. Embracing this diversity can be beneficial for community integration and overall harmony. Cultural adaptation involves respecting and learning from the traditions and practices of others, which can foster mutual understanding and cooperation.

For example, communal living may become more common, requiring everyone to respect shared spaces and resources. Learning about other cultures' communication styles, conflict resolution methods, and survival techniques can provide valuable insights and improve group cohesion. Adapting to these cultural differences can help build stronger, more resilient communities capable of facing the challenges of a post-apocalyptic world together.

Conflict Resolution

Disputes are inevitable in any society, especially in a high-stress, post-apocalyptic environment where resources are scarce. Effective conflict resolution techniques are essential to maintain stability and prevent violence. One effective approach is to establish clear, community-wide protocols for handling disputes. These protocols should prioritize peaceful negotiations and compromise.

When conflicts arise, encourage open communication where all parties can express their concerns without fear of retribution. Mediation by a neutral third party can also be helpful in reaching a fair resolution. Additionally, promoting empathy within the community—understanding and considering others' perspectives—can reduce tensions and foster a cooperative spirit.

Guideline: Establishing a structured process for conflict resolution can include regular community meetings where issues are discussed openly and resolutions are collectively agreed upon. This approach ensures transparency and fairness, helping to maintain trust and unity within the group.

Leadership Development

In times of crisis, effective leadership becomes even more critical. Developing strong leadership skills can enable individuals to guide their communities towards positive outcomes. Leadership in a post-apocalyptic world isn't just about commanding authority; it's about inspiring others, making informed decisions, and fostering a collaborative environment.

One key aspect of leadership is the ability to remain calm and composed under pressure. Demonstrating resilience and a clear vision can instill confidence in others. Leaders should also be good communicators, able to articulate plans and rally support from the community.

Guideline: Leadership development can be nurtured through training programs focused on critical thinking, problem-solving, and motivational skills. Encouraging individuals to take initiative in smaller tasks can build their confidence and prepare them for larger leadership roles.

Furthermore, ethical leadership is paramount. In a world where moral boundaries might blur, adhering to principles like fairness, integrity, and empathy can set a positive example and cultivate a trustworthy reputation. A leader who treats everyone with respect and values collective well-being over personal gain will likely attract loyal followers and foster a harmonious community.

Bartering and Trade in a Collapsed Economy

Establishing alternative economic systems in a post-apocalyptic world is crucial for survival. When traditional currencies lose value and societal structures collapse, communities must rely on mutual exchange and effective resource management to thrive. To achieve this goal, several key strategies should be embraced.

The first step is asset evaluation. In a post-apocalyptic scenario, the value of items changes dramatically. It's essential to identify which resources are most valuable for trade and bartering. Clean water, non-perishable food, medical supplies, and tools will likely top the list. Additionally, skills such as medical expertise, mechanical repair, and agricultural knowledge become highly valuable assets. By assessing and cataloging available resources, individuals and communities can better understand their trading potential and prioritize what they need versus what they can offer.

Next, developing negotiation skills becomes imperative. In an environment where formal markets no longer exist, the ability to negotiate effectively can mean the difference between acquiring essential supplies and going without. Practicing clear communication, understanding the needs and motivations of the other party, and being prepared to walk away are crucial components of successful negotiation. Role-playing scenarios with community members can help refine these skills. For example, one might simulate a situation where they need to trade a medical supply for food, practicing how they would present their case and what compromises they are willing to make.

Building fair trade networks is another essential strategy. Trust is the foundation of any sustainable trading system. In a post-apocalyptic world, creating small, trust-based trading communities can ensure more stable and reliable exchanges. Establishing transparent trading practices and adhering to agreed-upon rules helps build this trust. Regular community meetings to discuss and resolve any trade issues can also strengthen these networks. Such practices follow principles like those found in fair trade organizations, where transparency and accountability are paramount (*Our 10 Fair Trade Principles – World Fair Trade Organisation*, n.d.). Fair trading networks also benefit from clearly defined fair prices and wages. A fair price includes equitable negotiation between buyer and seller, reflecting the true value of goods or services exchanged. Similarly, fair wages ensure that individuals receive compensation adequate for a decent standard of living. These principles are vital for maintaining morale and ensuring everyone feels valued in the community.

Resource allocation is another critical aspect. Efficiently distributing resources to meet both individual and communal needs helps prevent shortages and conflict. Initially, it might involve setting up communal storage areas for essential goods like food and clean water. Rotating responsibilities for managing these stores can prevent hoarding and ensure fair distribution. It's also beneficial to create a plan for rationing during lean times. This could include detailed records of inventory and consumption patterns to predict future needs accurately and adjust allocations accordingly.

Communities should also focus on sustainable practices to extend the lifespan of their resources. Methods like crop rotation, conserving water, and regularly maintaining tools and equipment can significantly impact long-term sustainability. Teaching and sharing these techniques within the community ensures that everyone can contribute to and benefit from efficient resource management.

Incorporating teachings from established economic theories can further enhance post-apocalyptic trade systems. Traditional economic theories emphasize the benefits of free trade and the importance of balancing trade agreements with political realities (Krist, 2016). Although free trade in the conventional sense may not apply, its core tenet—optimizing production and exchange to benefit all parties—informs how communities can approach their new economic systems.

Moreover, understanding the concept of comparative advantage can aid in organizing which community members should focus on specific tasks based on their inherent skills and resources. For instance, someone skilled in agriculture should concentrate on farming, while another who excels in carpentry can focus on building and repairs. This division of labor maximizes efficiency and productivity, much like traditional economic models suggest.

It's also vital to adapt quickly to changing circumstances. As resources fluctuate or new threats emerge, being flexible and ready to adjust trading practices and resource allocation methods is crucial for ongoing survival. Communities should establish regular reviews of their economic strategies to ensure they remain effective and fair. Open forums where all members can voice concerns and suggest improvements can facilitate this adaptive process, ensuring everyone's needs are met while fostering unity and cooperation.

Establishing fair trading practices and ensuring no forced labor or child exploitation aligns with ethical standards even in a post-apocalyptic world. Ensuring that labor is voluntary and fairly compensated builds a stronger, more cohesive community. This adherence to ethical standards not only promotes fairness but also enhances the overall stability and functionality of the community.

Lastly, promoting non-discrimination, gender equity, and women's economic empowerment is fundamental. Ensuring equal access to resources and opportunities prevents social fractures and utilizes the full potential of every community member. Creating inclusive decision-making processes where everyone's voice is heard embeds these principles into the fabric of the community.

Travelling Safely Through Dangerous Areas

Navigating perilous environments while minimizing risks and ensuring personal safety is paramount in a post-apocalyptic world. Survival in such a drastically altered environment requires a strategic approach to risk assessment, stealth techniques, combating isolation, and vehicle maintenance.

The first step in managing these hazards is through effective risk assessment. Evaluating potential threats involves understanding the new landscape, identifying danger zones, and recognizing the signs of impending threats. For example, areas with dense vegetation may conceal predators or hostile groups, while open fields might expose you to sniper attacks or ambushes. Planning your routes accordingly can significantly reduce the chance of encountering unforeseen dangers. Always have a contingency plan and be aware of alternative paths in case your primary route becomes compromised. Carrying maps, whether physical or digital, and using them to constantly reassess your position and surroundings can be the difference between life and death.

Stealth techniques are another crucial component of navigating a dangerous world. Moving undetected can prevent unwanted confrontations and allow for smoother travel. Practicing stealth involves wearing non-reflective and noise-reducing clothing, moving slowly and deliberately, and avoiding well-trodden paths where others are likely to traverse. Techniques such as 'ghost walking'—placing your feet down gently and rolling from heel to toe—can minimize noise. Additionally, learning to use natural cover, such as trees and bushes, to hide or move unseen can provide substantial advantages. Training yourself to recognize and mimic the sounds of the environment can also help you blend in and avoid detection.

In a world where societal structures have broken down, combating isolation becomes not only a psychological challenge but a practical one. Establishing communication methods and emergency protocols during travel can enhance your chances of survival. Handheld radios, signal mirrors, and flares can be useful tools for maintaining contact with fellow survivors. Setting preset times and rendezvous points ensures that if you get separated, there is a clear plan to reunite. Developing simple codes or signals can convey messages quickly and discreetly, further aiding in maintaining security. Additionally, having an agreed-upon protocol for what to do if a member of your party is injured or lost is essential. This might include steps for immediate first aid, signaling for help, and making decisions about continuing the journey or waiting for rescue.

Maintaining transportation modes is essential for efficient and secure travel. Whether you're relying on vehicles, bicycles, or even makeshift carts, regular maintenance can prevent breakdowns at critical moments. Basic vehicle maintenance skills, such as changing tires, checking oil and coolant levels, and fixing minor mechanical issues, can significantly extend the usability of your transport. Knowing how to siphon fuel, identify common problems, and carry out quick fixes will keep your vehicle running longer. Equally important is securing your vehicle against theft or tampering; using steering wheel locks, removing vital engine components when parked, or even camouflaging your vehicle can deter would-be thieves.

Final Insights

Navigating a world with drastically altered societal norms requires an understanding of new social hierarchies, cultural adaptations, conflict resolution techniques, and effective leadership. Recognizing the power dynamics within your community and forming strategic alliances can ensure protection and resource access. Embracing diverse cultural practices fosters harmony and collaboration among survivors. Establishing clear protocols for peaceful conflict resolution maintains stability, while strong, ethical leadership inspires confidence and unity.

Thriving in such an environment demands both practical and interpersonal skills. Developing negotiation abilities and building trust-based trade networks enhance resource management and community cohesion. Practicing stealth techniques and maintaining transportation means optimize safety during travel. By applying these strategies, individuals and communities can better adapt to the challenges of a post-apocalyptic world, ensuring survival and fostering resilient, supportive networks.

Reference List

Brozović, D. (2023, January 1). *Societal collapse: A literature review* . Futures. https://doi.org/10.1016/j.futures.2022.103075

Evso guide-3rd-edition . (2018, October 5). SlideShare. https://www.slideshare.net/slideshow/evso-guide3rdedition/118258597

He, Q., Meng, X., & Qu, R. (2020, September 3). *Towards a Severity Assessment Method for Potential Cyber Attacks to Connected and Autonomous Vehicles* . Journal of Advanced Transportation. https://doi.org/10.1155/2020/6873273

Haferkamp, H., & Smelser, N. J. (2020). *Social Change and Modernity* . Cdlib.org. https://publishing.cdlib.org/ucpressebooks/view?docId=ft6000078s

Krist, W. (2016). *Chapter 3: Trade Agreements and Economic Theory* . Wilson Center. https://www.wilsoncenter.org/chapter-3-trade-agreements-and-economic-theory

Our 10 Fair Trade Principles – Word Fair Trade Organisation . (n.d.). World Fair Trade Organization. https://wfto.com/our-fair-trade-system/our-10-principles-of-fair-trade/

Chapter Eleven

Building and Leading Communities

Building and leading communities involves understanding the essential strategies for creating cohesive and resilient groups. Organizing like-minded individuals who share common goals forms the foundation of a strong community, providing a supportive network that can efficiently address challenges. By establishing trustworthy networks and fostering a culture of open communication, members can align their efforts towards shared objectives. This alignment not only strengthens the group's stability but also enhances its ability to function effectively under pressure.

This chapter delves into various organizational strategies that facilitate the creation of robust communities. Readers will explore how to identify and connect with individuals who share similar values, thus forming reliable networks built on trust. The importance of trust, especially during crises, is highlighted through practical examples and historical scenarios. Additionally, the chapter examines the value of leveraging diverse skills within the group, ensuring a well-rounded approach to problem-solving and resilience. Finally, it emphasizes the need for thorough screening processes to maintain group cohesion and prevent internal conflicts, ensuring that each member's contribution aligns with the community's overarching mission.

Finding like-minded individuals

Aligning with like-minded individuals is fundamental to building cohesive and resilient communities, especially in high-stakes scenarios such as natural disasters or societal breakdowns. When people come together based on shared values and goals, they can create a trustworthy network that serves as the backbone of any strong community. Building such networks should be at the forefront of your organizational strategy.

Creating Trustworthy Networks

At the heart of every resilient group lies a network built on trust. This process begins by identifying individuals who share similar beliefs and objectives. Doing so ensures that everyone is working towards common goals, making the network more stable and reliable. For example, if a group is unified by a commitment to emergency preparedness, each member will likely prioritize survival strategies and resource management. The volunteer fire services exemplify this principle; their members share a profound commitment to saving lives and property, which reinforces their resilience during crises (Consulting, 2023).

To establish these connections, it's important to facilitate open communication and regular interactions among potential group members. Holding community meetings, workshops, or social events can help individuals get to know each other better and build relationships rooted in mutual understanding and respect. This foundation of trust allows for seamless collaboration, even under pressure.

Building   Trust   During   Crises

Trust becomes especially crucial when the group faces a crisis. In these moments, the reliability and integrity of each member are tested. Effective teamwork hinges on this trust, enabling the group to coordinate their efforts efficiently. For instance, during a natural disaster, a well-coordinated team can quickly mobilize resources, delegate tasks, and provide support where it's needed most. Conversely, a lack of trust can lead to miscommunication, duplicated efforts, and unnecessary conflict, all of which can hinder the group's overall effectiveness.

Historical examples highlight the importance of trust in overcoming adversity. Consider the resilience demonstrated by communities facing devastating wildfires. Their success often hinges not just on individual bravery but also on a collective commitment and trust in one another (Consulting, 2023). Such trust fuels perseverance and enables the group to maintain cohesion under pressure.

Leveraging   Diverse   Skills

While aligning with like-minded individuals is essential, it is equally important to recognize the value of diversity within a group. Diversity brings a range of skills, perspectives, and problem-solving approaches, making the community more adaptable and innovative. For instance, in a survival scenario, having members skilled in different areas—such as medical care, engineering, agriculture, and tactical planning—can significantly enhance the group's chances of thriving.

In practical terms, leveraging diverse skills means ensuring that each member's unique abilities are recognized and utilized effectively. A diverse skill set allows the group to address a wide array of challenges. For example, while one member may excel in first aid and medical assistance, another might have expertise in mechanical repairs or food production. By pooling these varied skills, the group can develop comprehensive strategies for resource management, emergency response, and daily operations.

Screening   Potential   Members

To maintain a cohesive and functional group, it is essential to screen potential members thoroughly. This involves establishing guidelines for vetting individuals to ensure they align with the group's core values and objectives. Compatibility is key;

members should not only have the necessary skills but also share the same commitment to the group's goals.

When screening new members, consider conducting interviews, background checks, and trial periods. This process helps ensure that newcomers are equipped to contribute positively to the community. For instance, before admitting someone into a prepper group, you might assess their knowledge of survival techniques, their willingness to participate in collective activities, and their ability to work under stressful conditions.

One effective approach is to create a list of criteria that potential members must meet. These might include specific skills, a proven track record of reliability, and a demonstrated commitment to the group's mission. By adhering to these guidelines, the community can maintain its integrity and avoid internal conflicts that could undermine its resilience.

In conclusion, building and leading resilient communities require deliberate effort in aligning with like-minded individuals, fostering trust, embracing diversity, and carefully screening potential members. By creating trustworthy networks, emphasizing the importance of trust during crises, leveraging diverse skills, and setting clear vetting guidelines, communities can become robust and capable of facing any challenge.

Leadership roles and responsibilities

In any community, especially those preparing for extreme scenarios, having a defined leadership structure is crucial. Responsibilities must be clear for effective decision-making and coordination. Establishing hierarchies within the group provides clarity and ensures smooth operations.

Establishing Hierarchies

In a well-functioning group, everyone needs to know their role. Clarifying roles from the outset helps prevent confusion and inefficiencies. Leadership should identify key positions such as team leaders, emergency coordinators, and communication officers. Each position should have specific duties aligned with the group's overall goals. For instance, a team leader might oversee daily operations, while an emergency coordinator focuses on preparedness and response strategies.

A hierarchical structure doesn't mean authoritarian rule. Instead, it's about creating an organized system where everyone understands their responsibilities. A clear hierarchy can streamline processes, making it easier to execute plans efficiently. This structure should also be flexible enough to adapt to changing situations but stable enough to provide consistent direction.

Communication Protocols

Effective information dissemination is vital in any community, especially during emergencies. Structuring communication channels ensures that everyone stays informed and can act quickly when needed. The first step is to establish a reliable communication network. This could involve setting up group messaging systems, regular meetings, and emergency alert protocols.

Leaders should define how information flows within the group. For example, critical updates might be communicated through a chain of command, while general information can be shared via a group message. It's also essential to have backup communication methods in case primary systems fail. Regular drills and practice sessions can help ensure everyone knows how to use these channels effectively.

Transparency in communication builds trust within the group. Leaders should share not only what decisions are made but also why they are made. Providing context behind decisions helps members understand the rationale and reduces uncertainty. Open forums and feedback sessions can also foster a culture of openness and inclusivity.

Conflict Resolution Strategies

Disputes and disagreements are inevitable in any group, but how they're handled can significantly impact group cohesion. Developing conflict resolution strategies is essential to maintaining harmony. According to Henderson Community College, conflict management seeks to resolve disagreements with positive outcomes that satisfy all individuals involved or benefit the group. Properly managed conflict can promote team-building skills, critical thinking, new ideas, and alternative resolutions (Ronquillo et al., 2023).

Different conflicts require different approaches. An avoidance strategy might temporarily de-escalate a tense situation, but it won't solve underlying issues. On the other hand, a collaborative approach involves active listening, respectful communication, and open-mindedness, leading to a solution accepted by all parties involved. Collaborative tools like brainstorming sessions and mediation can be effective in resolving conflicts.

The group should have clear ground rules for conflict resolution. Before discussions begin, set rules for respectful communication. Ask members to engage in active listening without interruption. Having someone facilitate these sessions can keep conversations on track and focused on finding solutions. Follow-up mechanisms should be established to ensure that agreed-upon solutions are implemented.

Assigning Responsibilities Based on Skills and Experience

Effective leadership involves recognizing individual strengths and delegating tasks accordingly. Assigning responsibilities based on skills and experience not only enhances efficiency but also empowers members by placing them in roles where they can excel. Conducting a skills assessment can help identify who is best suited for specific tasks.

For example, someone with medical training could be responsible for health and first aid, while a person with experience in logistics might handle resource management. Matching roles to skills ensures that tasks are performed competently and that the group can rely on each other's expertise. This approach also encourages a sense of ownership and accountability, as members feel valued for their unique contributions.

Regular training and skill development sessions can help members improve their abilities and adapt to new challenges. Encouraging continuous learning fosters a culture of growth and resilience within the group. It's also beneficial to have cross-training so that multiple members can cover key roles if necessary.

Conclusion

Resource sharing and communal efforts

In the face of natural disasters, economic uncertainty, or societal breakdowns, effective community strategies for resource management and collaboration become vital. This section emphasizes the importance of pooling essential supplies, engaging in collaborative projects, promoting sustainability, and planning for emergency responses.

Pooling Essential Supplies

In times of crisis, access to vital resources can mean the difference between life and death. By pooling essential supplies—such as food, water, medical kits, and other necessities—the community ensures that everyone has equitable access during emergencies. Collective storage systems allow for a more organized and efficient distribution of these resources, preventing hoarding and ensuring that aid reaches those who need it most. This communal approach fosters a sense of solidarity and mutual responsibility.

For example, communities can establish central stockpiles where members contribute surplus supplies. These stockpiles are then managed by designated individuals or committees that monitor inventory levels and distribute goods fairly. Regular audits can help maintain transparency and trust within the community. Additionally, educational initiatives that teach members about the importance of contributing to and utilizing these pooled resources can enhance participation and compliance.

Collaborative Projects

Beyond sharing physical supplies, collaborating on joint initiatives can significantly benefit communities. Collaborative projects not only serve immediate needs but also contribute to skill development and community cohesion. For instance, setting up community gardens helps secure local food production while teaching valuable agricultural skills. Members can learn how to grow and harvest crops, recycle organic waste through composting, and support each other through the shared responsibility of tending to the garden.

Another example is organizing workshops on first aid, basic construction, or renewable energy installations. Such activities not only equip individuals with practical skills useful during emergencies but also strengthen the social fabric of the community as members work together towards common goals. Collaborative efforts in constructing shelters, repairing infrastructure, or developing alternative energy sources can also enhance the community's resilience to future crises.

Sustainable Practices

Sustainability plays a crucial role in long-term survival, particularly in challenging times. Communities must adopt practices that promote resource conservation and environmental stewardship. Encouraging sustainable living habits—like reducing waste, recycling, and conserving water—ensures that resources last longer and minimizes the ecological footprint.

For instance, implementing rainwater harvesting systems can provide an alternative water source during droughts or supply disruptions. Educating community members about the benefits of permaculture and organic farming can lead to more resilient agricultural practices that improve soil health and increase biodiversity. Hosting repair cafes where people bring broken items to be fixed instead of discarded reduces waste and promotes a culture of reuse and sustainability.

Moreover, integrating renewable energy solutions like solar panels, wind turbines, or biogas digesters into community infrastructure reduces dependence on external power sources and mitigates the impact of energy shortages. Communities can also explore options for local energy cooperatives, which enable collective ownership and management of energy resources, providing greater control and stability during crises.

Emergency Response Planning

Effective preparedness requires well-thought-out emergency response plans tailored to specific threats and vulnerabilities. Formulating strategies to address external threats involves a thorough assessment of potential risks—from natural disasters like hurricanes and earthquakes to man-made crises such as industrial accidents or civil unrest.

Communities should establish clear roles and responsibilities for members in emergency scenarios. Creating detailed evacuation plans, setting up communication protocols, and conducting regular drills ensures that everyone knows their part in responding to emergencies. Engaging professionals such as local firefighters, paramedics, and law enforcement in these preparations can provide valuable insights and training.

Furthermore, fostering strong partnerships with neighboring communities and external organizations enhances the overall capacity to respond effectively. Mutual aid agreements wherein communities pledge to assist each other during crises can extend support networks and resources beyond immediate geographical boundaries. This interconnectedness bolsters resilience and ensures a more coordinated response.

The concept of "active listening" becomes particularly important during crisis planning (Shmueli et al., 2020). Decision-makers must engage with community members to understand their concerns and priorities. This participatory approach empowers individuals, making them feel invested in the process and more likely to comply with established plans. Similarly, mediation strategies can help navigate conflicts that arise during planning, ensuring that diverse voices are heard and consensus is achieved.

Establishing conflict resolution policies is another critical aspect (María et al., 2023). Clear guidelines and mechanisms for addressing disputes prevent misunderstandings from escalating and disrupting emergency efforts. Training community leaders in mediation and negotiation techniques can equip them with the tools needed to manage disagreements constructively.

Bringing It All Together

In this chapter, we've explored strategies for forming cohesive and resilient groups through alignment with like-minded individuals, fostering trust, embracing diverse skills, and careful member screening. These elements form the foundation of any effective community, ensuring that everyone is united by common goals and values. We've seen how communication, regular interactions, and structured procedures build a reliable network capable of weathering crises. The significance of shared commitment has been highlighted through historical examples, underscoring the importance of mutual trust and collaboration.

We've also examined the benefits of leveraging diverse skills to enhance group adaptability and problem-solving capabilities. Screening potential members based on their skills and commitment ensures the integrity and functionality of the group. Deliberate efforts in these areas create robust communities prepared to face any challenge. By adopting these organizational strategies, you can build a proactive and resilient community ready to navigate the complexities of extreme scenarios.

Reference List

American Nurse Today. (2019, February 26). *Transforming culture through resiliency and teamwork - American Nurse* . American Nurse. https://www.myamericannurse.com/transforming-culture-resiliency-teamwork/

Control, V. (2024, January 30). *Conflict Resolution and Accountability through Collaborative Leadership* . Voltage Control. https://voltagecontrol.com/blog/conflict-resolution-and-accountability-through-collaborative-leadership/

Consulting, Q. (2023, November 8). *Does Teamwork Play a Role in Building Resilience? | Quay Consulting* . https://www.quayconsulting.com.au/news/does-teamwork-play-a-role-in-building-resilience/

María, A., Bodin, Ö., Nohrstedt, D., Plummer, R., Baird, J., & Summers, R. (2023, September 1). *Collaboration and individual performance during disaster response* . Global Environmental Change-Human and Policy Dimensions; Elsevier BV. https://doi.org/10.1016/j.gloenvcha.2023.102729

Ronquillo, Y., Ellis, V. L., & Toney-Butler, T. J. (2023, July 3). *Conflict management* . National Library of Medicine; StatPearls Publishing. https://www.ncbi.nlm.nih.gov/books/NBK470432/

Shmueli, D. F., Ozawa, C. P., & Kaufman, S. (2020, November). *Collaborative planning principles for disaster preparedness* . International Journal of Disaster Risk Reduction. https://doi.org/10.1016/j.ijdrr.2020.101981

Chapter Twelve

Mental and Emotional Resilience

Developing mental and emotional resilience is crucial for managing the challenges of high-stress situations. The ability to maintain composure, make sound decisions, and remain focused under pressure can significantly impact your overall well-being and effectiveness in navigating crises. Mental fortitude involves building strategies that enable you to handle stress with grace and determination. These coping mechanisms not only assist in surviving difficult moments but also in emerging stronger and more resilient from them.

In this chapter, we delve into various techniques designed to enhance your mental and emotional resilience. We'll explore effective stress management methods such as controlled breathing exercises and physical activity, which help maintain calmness and clarity during high-pressure scenarios. Reflection and journaling practices will be discussed as powerful tools for introspection and self-awareness. Additionally, we will cover ways to simplify your routine by eliminating unnecessary stressors and emphasize the importance of building a solid support system. By incorporating these strategies into your daily life, you can develop a robust mental framework to tackle any adversity.

Stress Management Techniques

During a crisis, managing stress and anxiety becomes crucial for maintaining mental and emotional resilience. Stress can affect your ability to think clearly and make sound decisions, so finding effective methods to cope is essential. Here, we explore several strategies that can help you stay calm, focused, and resourceful during high-stress situations.

One of the most effective methods for managing stress involves learning to control your breathing. When faced with a stressful situation, your body's natural response is to breathe rapidly and shallowly. This can worsen feelings of panic and anxiety. Practicing deep breathing exercises can help regulate your breath, reduce tension, and promote relaxation. Controlled breathing techniques, such as diaphragmatic or abdominal breathing, involve inhaling deeply through the nose, allowing your abdomen to expand, and exhaling slowly through the mouth. Studies show that these techniques can lower cortisol levels in the body, which is a hormone associated with stress (Russo et al., 2017). Using deep breathing exercises consistently can help you maintain focus and keep panic at bay during crises.

Engaging in physical exercise is another potent method for alleviating stress and anxiety. Physical activity triggers the release of endorphins, which are chemicals in the brain that act as natural painkillers and mood elevators. Regular exercise can improve your overall mood and provide a sense of accomplishment, making it easier to manage stressful situations. Various forms of exercise, such as walking, running, yoga, strength training, or even dancing, can be beneficial. For instance, a brisk walk in nature can not only give you a break from a stressful environment but also clear your mind and refresh your perspective. The key is to find an activity you enjoy, making it more likely that you'll stick with it. As research indicates, exercise is linked to better mental health and lower stress levels (Sharma et al., 2006).

Reflecting on past experiences can offer significant insights and emotional relief during times of crisis. Taking time to analyze what you've been through allows you to identify patterns, understand your reactions, and find lessons that can be applied in future situations. Reflection can be done through various means, such as talking to someone you trust, meditating, or simply spending quiet moments in thought. By reflecting on your experiences, you gain a deeper understanding of yourself and your coping mechanisms, which can empower you to handle new challenges more effectively.

Journaling is another powerful tool for managing stress and anxiety. Writing down your thoughts and emotions helps to externalize your worries, making them less overwhelming. It serves as a form of self-discovery and introspection, where you can explore your feelings, track your progress, and identify triggers that cause stress. Journaling can take many forms, from daily diaries to gratitude journals, where you list things you're thankful for each day. This practice not only helps to declutter your mind but also fosters a positive outlook. Studies have shown that people who journal regularly experience lower levels of stress and greater emotional clarity (Scott, 2023). Making journaling a habit can significantly contribute to your mental well-being and resilience.

Additionally, it's important to recognize and eliminate sources of unnecessary stress. Sometimes, reducing stress involves cutting out activities or habits that contribute to your anxiety. This might mean limiting your exposure to negative news, taking breaks from social media, reducing caffeine and alcohol intake, or reassessing your to-do list to ensure it's realistic. Simplifying your daily routine can free up mental space and energy, making it easier to deal with unavoidable stressors (Scott, 2023).

Building a support system is equally vital for managing stress during crises. Having friends, family, or colleagues to talk to can provide emotional comfort and practical advice. Social support helps to buffer the effects of stress by offering a sense of belonging and reassurance. If your existing network isn't providing the support you need, consider expanding it by joining groups or communities related to your interests. Even professional help from therapists or counselors can be invaluable in developing effective coping strategies.

Practicing Mindfulness and Meditation

Introducing mindfulness and meditation practices to cultivate inner peace and focus is essential for developing mental and emotional resilience. Mindfulness, the practice of being fully present in the moment, has been shown to reduce anxiety and promote mental clarity. By focusing on the here and now, individuals can prevent their minds from wandering into stressful thoughts about the past or future. This technique helps ground them and provides a sense of calmness even during high-stress situations.

Regular meditation can enhance concentration and emotional stability. Studies have shown that consistent meditation practice leads to improved attention span and better cognitive functions. For example, Ortner, Kilner, and Zelazo (2007) found that participants with mindfulness meditation experience had reduced emotional interference and higher psychological well-being (Keng et al., 2011). Moreover, meditation fosters emotional regulation by enabling practitioners to observe their feelings without judgment, thus reducing impulsive reactions and fostering a more composed demeanor.

Visualization exercises are another powerful tool within meditation practices that can boost confidence and optimism in challenging situations. Visualization involves creating vivid mental images of desired outcomes or experiences, which can mentally prepare an individual for real-world scenarios. This technique is especially useful in survival situations where maintaining a positive and determined mindset is crucial. By repeatedly visualizing success, the brain becomes familiar with the process, making it easier to achieve the same results in reality.

Practicing visualization techniques aids in building mental resilience by training the mind to handle stress and uncertainty. When individuals visualize themselves successfully navigating difficulties, they build the mental fortitude needed to carry those skills into actual events. Visualization also helps in breaking down complex goals into manageable steps, reinforcing the belief that they can overcome obstacles one step at a time.

One effective way to incorporate mindfulness into daily life is through simple mindful breathing exercises. These can be practiced anywhere and at any time, making them accessible tools for immediate stress reduction. By gradually increasing the duration and regularity of these sessions, individuals can cultivate a habit that significantly boosts their mental health and resilience.

Another meditation practice beneficial for mental resilience is the body scan meditation. This technique involves mentally scanning oneself from head to toe to observe any discomfort, tension, or sensations. The practice enhances self-awareness and helps release physical stress, contributing to overall emotional stability. It is particularly useful after long or strenuous activities that may leave the body and mind feeling drained.

Transcendental meditation (TM), which involves silently repeating a specific mantra, can also be highly effective. TM has been widely studied and is known for reducing stress and enhancing self-awareness. Students, in particular, have found this form of meditation helpful for improving academic performance and reducing exam-related stress. Research indicates reductions in physiological arousal markers like oxygen consumption and respiratory rate among TM practitioners, demonstrating its calming effects (Meditation for College Students: 6 Best Types to Practice — Calm Blog, n.d.).

Guided visualization, where a scenario is described to lead one's thoughts, serves as another excellent method for managing anxiety and promoting relaxation. This type of meditation instills a positive mental shift and can act as a rehearsal for overcoming upcoming challenges, such as public speaking or high-pressure meetings. Regular practice of guided visualization strengthens mental pathways associated with confidence and composure.

Loving-kindness meditation, which focuses on developing compassion and goodwill toward oneself and others, is another valuable technique. This practice has been found to enhance emotional resilience and improve social relationships. By consistently sending out positive intentions, practitioners can maintain a more optimistic outlook, which is vital during tough times.

Focused attention meditation, where concentration is placed on a single object or thought, helps train the mind to avoid distractions. This technique is particularly useful in situations requiring sustained attention and focus. Over time, practicing focused attention can significantly improve one's ability to remain calm and collected under pressure.

To integrate these practices seamlessly into daily life, creating a conducive environment for meditation is crucial. Finding a quiet space free from distractions allows for deeper concentration and more effective meditation sessions. Establishing a regular routine, whether starting with just a few minutes each day or linking meditation to everyday habits like brushing teeth, can help embed these practices into one's lifestyle.

Incorporating mindfulness and meditation into your routine doesn't require complex preparations. Simple steps like setting realistic goals, understanding that the mind will wander, and using guided meditations can make the journey smoother. Apps and online resources provide structured guidance, helping beginners navigate the initial stages of their practice.

Mindful breathing exercises can offer quick mental resets when extended meditation isn't feasible. Techniques like the 4-7-8 method or box breathing can be employed before exams or during study breaks to quickly calm the mind and restore focus. Regular use of these exercises conditions the brain to manage stress more efficiently.

Fostering Positive Attitudes

Encouraging a positive mindset and optimistic outlook during tough times is crucial for developing mental and emotional resilience. During high-stress situations, maintaining a constructive perspective can significantly impact how we cope and overcome challenges. One effective way to promote such a mindset is through the practice of gratitude.

Expressing gratitude can improve mental well-being and resilience. When we acknowledge the good things in our lives, we shift our focus from problems to blessings. This shift enables us to handle stress more effectively by creating a sense of hope and motivation. Studies show that gratitude fosters adaptive coping mechanisms. By managing positive emotions like satisfaction, happiness, and pleasure, it enhances our emotional resilience and builds inner strength to combat stress (Gloria & Steinhardt, 2016). In stressful scenarios, reflecting on what we are grateful for can ground us and provide clarity amidst chaos. Simple practices such as keeping a gratitude journal or making a mental list of things we're thankful for daily can start this transformative process. Consistency in these practices helps build a habit that fortifies our mental state over time.

Positive self-talk is another powerful tool for fostering a positive mindset. The way we speak to ourselves influences our confidence and motivation, particularly in challenging situations. For example, if you're feeling nervous about speaking up during an important meeting, practice saying, "My input is valuable and deserves to be shared," or, "My work performance does not define my worth." Although this may seem strange initially, with practice, you can train your brain to overwrite negative thoughts with positive ones, reducing worry and increasing your chances of success (*Enhance Your Life with Applied Positive Psychology | Penn LPS Online*, 2023). Creating a habit of affirming positive beliefs about oneself can turn into a reliable source of inner strength that helps to navigate through adversity.

Being adaptable is an essential trait for navigating challenges and setbacks effectively. Adaptability means being open to change and willing to adjust one's approach when faced with new circumstances. This skill is vital in unpredictable and high-pressure environments where rigid plans often fail. By embracing flexibility, individuals can find new solutions to problems and quickly recover from setbacks. Adaptability requires a willingness to learn and grow from experiences rather than seeing them as insurmountable obstacles.

Cultivating adaptability fosters a positive mindset, especially in adverse conditions. When we view challenges as opportunities to evolve, we become more equipped to handle them without falling into despair. It allows us to maintain a proactive rather than a reactive stance towards difficulties. To cultivate adaptability, consider practicing scenarios where you might have to make quick decisions or alter your plans. This could involve small exercises like taking a different route to work or trying out new problem-solving strategies. Over time, these small changes can help build the mental flexibility needed for more significant challenges.

Gratitude practices can be straightforward yet profoundly impactful in building emotional resilience. Meditation and breath control, for instance, set the foundation for a robust gratitude practice. Starting any gratitude exercise with a brisk meditation and deep breathing session can alleviate immediate stress and prepare the mind for deeper reflection. This practice centers the mind and helps gather focus, allowing feelings of thankfulness to surface more naturally. Regular meditation helps create a calm mental state, providing the perfect backdrop for gratitude exercises.

Creating a gratitude list is another simple yet effective practice. Much like a gratitude journal, a gratitude list helps bring blessings and supportive people to your attention. Take some time each day to note down names of individuals who have supported you through tough times, along with specific instances where their help made a difference. Reflecting on this list regularly can reignite feelings of gratitude and strengthen emotional resilience. Once your list is complete, consider extending your gratitude by sending thank-you notes to those individuals. These notes can be short and sincere, expressing genuine appreciation. Sending such messages not only reinforces your own feelings of gratitude but also strengthens social bonds, which are critical during challenging times.

Reminiscence meditation is yet another method to nurture gratitude. By recalling past events where you successfully overcame challenges, you can tap into feelings of resilience and confidence. This form of meditation brings a sense of accomplishment and positivity, reinforcing your ability to tackle future adversities. By remembering past successes, even small ones, you bolster your belief in overcoming current and future challenges.

Bringing It All Together

In this chapter, we delved into various techniques to boost mental fortitude in high-stress situations. We explored methods like controlled breathing, which helps manage physical responses to stress by promoting relaxation and focus. Physical exercise emerged as a potent way to alleviate anxiety through endorphin release, enhancing mood and providing a sense of accomplishment. Reflective practices such as journaling and analyzing past experiences were also highlighted as crucial tools for gaining insights and emotional relief.

We further examined the importance of simplifying daily routines to cut down on unnecessary stressors and the value of building a supportive network of friends, family, or colleagues. These strategies collectively work to create a foundation of resilience. Incorporating these techniques into your routine can significantly improve your ability to handle crises effectively. Remember, developing mental and emotional resilience is an ongoing process that requires consistent practice and self-awareness.

Reference List

Chowdhury, M. R. (2019, April 9). *The Neuroscience of Gratitude and Effects on the Brain* . PositivePsychology.com. https://positivepsychology.com/neuroscience-of-gratitude/

Enhance your life with applied positive psychology | Penn LPS Online . (2023, May 15). Lpsonline.sas.upenn.edu. https://lpsonline.sas.upenn.edu/features/enhance-your-life-applied-positive-psychology

Keng, S. L., Smoski, M. J., & Robins, C. J. (2011). *Effects of Mindfulness on Psychological health: a Review of Empirical Studies* . Clinical Psychology Review. https://doi.org/10.1016/j.cpr.2011.04.006

Meditation for college students: 6 best types to practice — Calm Blog . (n.d.). Calm Blog. Retrieved July 29, 2024, from https://www.calm.com/blog/meditation-for-college-students

Robinson, L., & Smith, M. (2023, October 11). *Stress Management* . HelpGuide. https://www.helpguide.org/articles/stress/stress-management.htm

Scott, E. (2023, September 13). *18 Highly Effective Stress Relievers* . Verywell Mind; Verywellmind. https://www.verywellmind.com/tips-to-reduce-stress-3145195

Chapter Thirteen

Continuous Learning and Improvement

Continuous Learning and Improvement

Adopting a mindset of continuous learning and improvement is key to thriving in uncertain times. In the ever-changing landscape of emergency preparedness, the ability to stay informed about new survival strategies can make all the difference. As we face natural disasters, economic instability, or societal upheavals, the need to adapt becomes even more pressing. Continuous learning empowers individuals to refine their skills, embrace innovative approaches, and enhance their overall resilience. By fostering ongoing growth and adaptability, you equip yourself to confront challenges head-on and navigate through crises with confidence.

This chapter delves into various aspects of adopting a mindset geared toward continuous learning and improvement. You'll explore the importance of staying updated on evolving survival techniques, such as alternative shelter methods and advanced food storage solutions. The chapter also discusses the value of learning tactical maneuvers for evacuation, ensuring safety during unpredictable disaster scenarios. Additionally, it emphasizes the necessity of participating in online forums, survival blogs, workshops, and local training sessions to exchange knowledge and gain hands-on experience. By the end of this chapter, you'll have a deeper understanding of how to integrate these practices into your survival strategy, enabling you to remain adaptable and prepared for whatever challenges may arise.

Staying Informed about New Survival Strategies

Understanding the importance of staying updated on evolving survival techniques and strategies is crucial for anyone serious about preparedness. In a world where conditions can change rapidly, being able to adapt to new information and methodologies can make a significant difference in an emergency.

Researching alternative shelter methods is an essential area of ongoing learning. Traditional shelters like tents, cabins, and makeshift lean-tos are reliable but may not always suit various environments or circumstances. Innovative designs such as geodesic domes offer strength and stability while being relatively easy to assemble. Additionally, exploring the potential of bio-materials like mycelium, which can grow around a framework to form a solid structure, could provide eco-friendly shelter options. Understanding how to utilize natural landscape features effectively, such as digging into hillsides for protection from elements or using tree canopies for camouflage, can further enhance your ability to create functional and discreet shelters. (*Urban Survival Techniques: 11 Ways to Master - Natureofthenorth.co,* 2024)

Exploring advanced food storage techniques is another key aspect of adapting to evolving survival strategies. Modern methods of preserving food can significantly extend shelf life and save space, crucial for long-term sustainability. Vacuum sealing can keep perishables fresh by removing air that causes spoilage. Freeze-drying technology, though requiring some initial investment, allows you to store lightweight, nutrient-rich foods that can be rehydrated quickly. Learning how to build root cellars can take advantage of naturally cool temperatures underground to preserve produce without electricity. Incorporating these methods helps ensure you have a variety of preserved foods available, maximizing your nutritional intake over time. Additionally, understanding fermentation processes—such as making sauerkraut or kimchi—not only preserves vegetables but also boosts their probiotic content, promoting gut health. (*Be Ready, Not Scared: Creating a Practical SHTF Plan,* n.d.)

Learning tactical maneuvers for evacuation is vital for ensuring safety during unpredictable disaster scenarios. Efficient evacuation requires more than just knowing routes; it involves mastering stealth movement and strategic positioning. Practicing low-light navigation can be invaluable for nighttime evacuations, minimizing the chance of detection. Understanding how to use natural cover and shadows to remain unseen can help you move undetected during crises. It's also helpful to practice moving silently and swiftly through various terrains, whether urban or rural, to be prepared regardless of the environment. Developing skills in reading maps and using compasses ensures you can find the safest paths even when digital tools fail. Additionally, understanding basic self-defense tactics improves your chances of protecting yourself against potential threats during evacuation scenarios.

Incorporating these teachings requires dedication to continual learning and adaptation. With new advancements and research emerging regularly, staying informed is a dynamic process. Online forums, survival blogs, and workshops offer platforms to exchange knowledge and experiences with others in the community. Participating in local meetups or training sessions hosted by experts provides hands-on experience, reinforcing theoretical knowledge with practical application. Books authored by seasoned survivalists often contain valuable insights drawn from real-life scenarios, offering lessons and strategies that can be directly applied.

Learning from Past Experiences

Leveraging past experiences is a crucial aspect of continuous learning and improvement in survival situations. The process begins with analyzing previous survival scenarios, whether personal or historical. By reflecting on these events, individuals can uncover both strengths and weaknesses in their preparedness strategies. For example, considering how communities survived during natural disasters like hurricanes or wildfires can reveal common effective practices such as stockpiling essential supplies or having a reliable communication plan. Similarly, personal experiences, such as getting through a severe winter storm, can help identify what worked well and what didn't, providing valuable insights for future preparedness.

To make the most out of these reflections, it's important to document survival insights diligently. Keeping a detailed journal of survival experiences captures successful strategies and areas needing improvement. This documentation serves as a personal reference that can be revisited whenever necessary. Moreover, sharing these journals with others fosters mutual learning. Fellow preppers and survivalists can benefit from each other's documented experiences, broadening their knowledge and enhancing group readiness. For instance, if someone documents the success of using solar-powered equipment during a prolonged power outage, others can consider integrating similar tools into their plans.

After-Action Reviews (AARs) are another invaluable tool for leveraging past experiences. These reviews involve evaluating performance following a survival event through structured debrief sessions. During an AAR, participants discuss what actions were taken, what outcomes occurred, and why certain decisions were made. This process helps identify which strategies were effective and which were not, paving the way for corrective measures. For instance, a debrief after evacuating due to a wildfire might reveal that communication between family members was poor, suggesting a need to establish better protocols for future emergencies.

Conducting AARs offers numerous benefits. According to McCarthy et al. (2023), simulated training videos of AARs support social and inclusive learning, showing how such reviews can help develop a shared understanding of events and prevention strategies among the participants. This collaborative learning approach ensures that everyone involved gains a comprehensive view of the situation and contributes to devising more effective plans for the future. It encourages open discussion and critical thinking, essential components in refining survival tactics.

Reflecting on historical survival scenarios also provides a wealth of knowledge. Take, for example, the Great Depression era; many families learned to become self-sufficient by growing their own food and repurposing household items. Modern survivalists can draw inspiration from these practices, adapting them to contemporary settings. Additionally, reviewing military survival strategies, like those used by soldiers during World War II, highlights the importance of resilience and resourcefulness, essential traits for enduring extreme circumstances.

Documenting these insights meticulously cannot be overstated. Using a personal journal to record experiences allows for detailed tracking of what went right and wrong. This practice also promotes introspection and continuous improvement. For instance, documenting a camping trip where unexpected weather changes occurred could highlight the necessity of packing adaptable clothing and extra gear. Sharing such documented experiences within a community magnifies the collective learning, creating a repository of practical knowledge that everyone can access and learn from.

Implementing After-Action Reviews anchors this reflective process in structured analysis. By breaking down the events step-by-step, participants can understand the rationale behind their actions and the resulting consequences. For example, an AAR conducted after a flood evacuation might expose flaws in the initial evacuation route chosen, prompting the development of alternative routes in subsequent plans. Darling et al. (2001) note that debriefing sessions fundamentally rely on integrating individual and collective functions, underscoring the value of combining personal progress with team performance. This holistic approach ensures that both personal experiences and group dynamics are considered, leading to more robust and well-rounded survival strategies.

Furthermore, conducting AARs should not be limited to major survival events. Routine drills and minor incidents provide excellent opportunities for review and improvement. Regularly engaging in AARs conditions individuals to think critically about their actions and continuously seek better methods. For instance, a routine fire drill at home could lead to discovering faster evacuation routes or more efficient ways of gathering essential items quickly. This ongoing cycle of action, reflection, and adjustment fortifies preparedness plans, making them more resilient over time.

Establishing guidelines for effective documentation and AARs further enhances their utility. When documenting survival insights, it's crucial to include specific details such as the context of the situation, actions taken, outcomes achieved, and lessons learned. This thoroughness ensures that documented experiences are comprehensive and actionable. Creating a standardized format for these records can facilitate easier sharing and comparison with others' experiences. Similarly, setting clear objectives and rules for conducting AARs ensures these sessions remain focused and productive. For instance, designating a leader to guide the discussion and keeping sessions time-bound can prevent digressions and maintain a forward-looking perspective.

Embracing these practices fosters a culture of continuous learning and adaptability. Analyzing past scenarios, meticulous documentation, and conducting structured AARs synergize to create a robust framework for improving survival strategies. Each element reinforces the other, driving an iterative process of growth and betterment. Whether preparing for natural disasters, economic upheavals, or societal breakdowns, leveraging past experiences equips individuals and communities with the knowledge and skills required to face future challenges with confidence and resilience.

In conclusion, taking a proactive approach to learning from past experiences is indispensable for anyone serious about emergency preparedness and survival. By analyzing previous scenarios, documenting insights, and conducting thorough after-action reviews, we can transform our experiences into powerful tools for future decision-making and strategy development. This ongoing cycle of reflection and improvement not only enhances individual readiness but also strengthens the collective resilience of survivalist communities. Through diligent practice and thoughtful evaluation, we can continuously refine our preparedness strategies, ensuring we are always ready to adapt and thrive, no matter what challenges may come our way.

Regularly Updating Survival Plans

Emphasizing the importance of continually revisiting and revising survival plans is crucial to ensuring preparedness in extreme scenarios. To effectively adapt to changing circumstances, preppers should focus on three main strategies: conducting periodic plan reviews, testing plan execution, and incorporating lessons learned.

Conducting periodic plan reviews is the first step toward maintaining an effective survival strategy. Establishing a regular schedule for reassessing your survival plans allows you to incorporate new information, technologies, and evolving threats into your preparations. For instance, advancements in portable water filtration systems or solar-powered gadgets could significantly improve your ability to sustain yourself during a disaster. Reviewing and updating your plans quarterly or biannually ensures that they remain relevant and comprehensive.

A practical approach to plan reviews involves preparing a checklist of critical elements within your survival plan. Items on this list might include communication methods, emergency contacts, shelter locations, food and water supplies, and medical resources. By systematically evaluating each aspect, you can identify potential gaps or outdated practices. Additionally, keeping abreast of any changes in local and national emergency protocols can inform necessary adjustments in your plans. This systematic reassessment not only strengthens your preparedness but also provides peace of mind.

Testing plan execution is another essential component of effective preparedness. Running drills and simulations helps evaluate team coordination, communication, and the viability of your plans under different disaster scenarios. Just as fire drills teach individuals how to evacuate buildings safely, survival drills prepare you and your team to respond effectively during real emergencies.

When organizing drills, it is beneficial to create a variety of scenarios that mimic potential threats such as natural disasters, economic collapse, or societal breakdowns. For example, you might simulate an earthquake to practice rapid evacuation and securing safe locations. Another drill could involve a prolonged power outage, ensuring everyone knows how to access and utilize backup power sources, preserve perishable supplies, and maintain communications. These realistic exercises enable you to gauge the efficiency of your procedures and pinpoint weaknesses.

In addition to traditional drills, consider incorporating technology-based simulations. Virtual reality (VR) tools can provide immersive experiences of various disaster situations, enhancing your ability to practice decision-making and problem-solving in high-stress environments. By running these drills periodically, you can ensure that all involved parties remain proficient and confident in executing the survival plan.

Incorporating lessons learned from both training exercises and real-life events is vital for continuous improvement. The feedback gathered from drills reveals what works well and what requires refinement. After each exercise, conduct debrief sessions where participants can discuss their experiences, share observations, and suggest improvements. This collaborative approach fosters a deeper understanding of the plan's strengths and vulnerabilities.

Furthermore, analyzing real-life events, whether personal experiences or incidents from other communities, offers valuable insights. For instance, examining how well-prepared communities handled hurricanes or wildfires can highlight effective strategies and common pitfalls. Documenting these insights and integrating them into your survival plan enhances its robustness. This iterative process mirrors the principles of the National Preparedness System, which emphasizes metrics-based assessments and feedback mechanisms to measure progress and identify best practices (The White House, 2006).

Enhancing equipment lists based on lessons learned is another critical aspect of plan revision. If drills reveal that certain tools or supplies are missing or inadequate, update your inventory accordingly. This might involve adding more first-aid kits, acquiring additional water storage solutions, or investing in improved communication devices. Similarly, update your list of emergency contacts to ensure it includes current information for family members, friends, local authorities, and emergency services.

Maintaining a record of all revisions and updates is essential for transparency and accountability. Keeping detailed logs of changes made to the survival plan allows you to track progress over time and ensures that everyone involved is aware of the latest protocols. This documentation can be particularly useful when onboarding new team members or during joint exercises with other prepper groups.

Effective communication is another cornerstone of successful survival planning. Establish clear communication channels and protocols to be used during emergencies. These might include designated rally points, code words, and backup methods such as satellite phones or two-way radios. Regularly test these communication systems to ensure they function correctly and that all team members are comfortable using them.

Building a culture of continuous improvement within your prepper community fosters resilience and adaptability. Encourage open dialogue about what needs improvement and celebrate successes in executing drills effectively. This ongoing commitment to learning and adapting reinforces the mindset of ongoing growth and adaptability essential for thriving amidst uncertainty.

Final Thoughts

Adopting a mindset of ongoing growth and adaptability is essential for anyone serious about preparedness. It begins with staying informed about the latest survival strategies, from researching innovative shelter designs using geodesic domes and bio-materials to mastering advanced food preservation techniques like vacuum sealing and freeze-drying. Regularly updating your knowledge ensures that you can adapt to changing conditions swiftly and effectively. This constant learning process involves more than just gathering information; it includes practical application through hands-on activities such as participating in workshops, training sessions, and local meetups hosted by experts. By actively engaging in these opportunities, you not only expand your skill set but also build a network of like-minded individuals who can share valuable insights and experiences.

Incorporating tactical maneuvers and conducting after-action reviews further enhances your adaptability. Practicing evacuation drills under various scenarios, such as natural disasters or prolonged power outages, helps refine your response strategies. After each exercise, reviewing the outcomes and discussing what worked well and what didn't provides critical feedback for improvement. Documenting these insights in a journal allows you to track your progress and make necessary adjustments over time. Sharing this knowledge with others fosters collective resilience, enabling the entire community to benefit from shared experiences. Through continuous learning, documenting personal and group experiences, and refining strategies based on real-life events, you can ensure that your preparedness plans remain robust and effective.

Reference List

Be Ready, Not Scared: Creating a Practical SHTF Plan . (n.d.). MIRA Safety. Retrieved July 29, 2024, from https://www.mirasafety.com/blogs/news/shtf-plan

Darling, M. J., & Parry, C. S. (2001). *After-action reviews: Linking reflection and planning in a learning practice* . Reflections The SoL Journal , 3(2), 64-72. https://doi.org/10.1162/15241730152695252

Fire safety training review: Startup Survival Skills: What Fire Drills Teach Us About Business . (n.d.). FasterCapital. Retrieved July 29, 2024, from https://fastercapital.com/content/Fire-safety-training-review--Startup-Survival-Skills--What-Fire-Drills-Teach-Us-About-Business.html

McCarthy, S. E., Hogan, C., Jenkins, L., Schwanberg, L., Williams, D. J., Mellon, L., Walsh, A., Keane, T., & Rafter, N. (2023, August 1). *Videos of simulated after action reviews: a training resource to support social and inclusive learning from patient safety events.* Videos of Simulated after Action Reviews: A Training Resource to Support Social and Inclusive Learning from Patient Safety Events. https://psnet.ahrq.gov/issue/videos-simulated-after-action-reviews-training-resource-support-social-and-inclusive-learning

The White House. (2006, February 23). *Hurricane Katrina: Lessons Learned - Chapter Six: Transforming National Preparedness* . Archives.gov. https://georgewbush-whitehouse.archives.gov/reports/katrina-lessons-learned/chapter6.html

Urban survival techniques: 11 Ways to Master - natureofthenorth.co . (2024, February 20). https://natureofthenorth.co/basics/urban-survival-techniques/

Chapter Fourteen

Conclusion

As we draw this guide to a close, it's essential to revisit the core lessons that have been shared. Throughout these pages, you've amassed crucial knowledge about understanding various catastrophic events, be they natural disasters, economic downturns, or societal breakdowns. You've learned how to craft thorough survival plans tailored to different scenarios, ensuring you and your loved ones are safeguarded against the unexpected. Securing essential supplies, from food and water to medical supplies and tools, has been emphasized as a non-negotiable part of preparedness. Just as vital is the development of skills—such as first aid, navigation, self-defense, and resource management—that empower you to handle the uncertainty with confidence.

The concepts we've discussed are not merely theoretical; they form a practical blueprint for building a resilient life in the face of adversity. This journey you've undertaken isn't about fostering fear but rather cultivating a deep-seated sense of empowerment. Preparation is an act of hope—it signifies your belief in a future where you can overcome challenges and thrive despite them. The time and effort you've invested in learning and planning reflect a commitment to a proactive mindset. Every drill, every piece of equipment, and every strategy contributes to a robust safety net designed to catch you when chaos strikes.

Now that you're equipped with extensive knowledge, the next step is to translate that into consistent action. Action transforms potential into reality. It's imperative to regularly review and update your survival strategies, taking into consideration any new information, technological advancements, or changing circumstances in your environment. Engage in practical drills periodically to ensure that both you and your family are familiar with what to do when a real emergency occurs. Practicing these drills turns your plan from a static document into a dynamic response system capable of adapting to live situations.

Staying informed about new survival techniques and strategies is equally important. The field of emergency preparedness is continually evolving, with innovators constantly developing new tools and methodologies to enhance survival odds. By keeping abreast of these developments, you stay ahead of the curve, positioning yourself to better handle whatever comes your way. Whether it's through online forums, community workshops, or survivalist networks, continuous learning is crucial. Always remember that preparedness is an ongoing process, one that requires vigilance and adaptability.

Beyond the individual level, the significance of mental resilience cannot be overstated. In times of crisis, maintaining a positive attitude can significantly influence outcomes. Mental fortitude acts as a stabilizer amidst the turmoil, allowing you to make sound decisions under pressure. Building mental resilience involves fostering a mindset that views challenges as opportunities for growth. Positivity, coupled with practical readiness, equips you with a holistic approach to navigating crises.

Community plays a pivotal role during adversities. While individual preparedness is essential, there's unmatched strength in numbers. Draw upon the power of community by forming or joining local preparedness groups. These groups provide a support system where resources, skills, and knowledge can be shared. In times of need, having a network of like-minded individuals can mean the difference between mere survival and thriving. Working together creates a formidable force, capable of withstanding even the most daunting challenges. Remember, resilience is amplified through unity.

Reflect on the journey you've embarked on. Each step taken towards becoming prepared has contributed to a larger path of transformation. From the initial decision to delve into preparedness to the comprehensive plans and skill-building exercises you've engaged in, every action marks significant progress. Your journey underscores a profound dedication to safeguarding your future. Thank you for entrusting this guide to assist you along the way.

This venture into preparedness cultivates more than just survival skills—it fosters leadership. As you move forward, empowered by the knowledge and capabilities you've developed, consider how you can take on a leadership role within your community. Share your insights, mentor others, and advocate for widespread preparedness. In doing so, you contribute to building a resilient society where collective strength arises from individual commitments.

In conclusion, may this guide serve as a foundation from which you continue to grow and excel in the realm of preparedness. Embrace each opportunity to learn and adapt, remaining steadfast in your resolve to protect what matters most. Let your actions be guided by the principles of vigilance, resilience, and unity. When faced with uncertainty, stand tall knowing that you have equipped yourself not just to survive, but to lead and thrive. The road ahead may be fraught with challenges, but armed with preparation, there is no obstacle you cannot overcome.

Thank you for embarking on this journey towards readiness. Your dedication to preparedness reflects a powerful commitment to securing a stable and hopeful future. May you continue to rise above every challenge, emerging stronger and more resilient with each step.

www.ingramcontent.com/pod-product-compliance
Lightning Source LLC
Chambersburg PA
CBHW070749250726
48662CB00004B/1715

9 798334 513587